# PUBLIC SPEAKING WITH CONFIDENCE

## CONQUER ANXIETY, CAPTIVATE ANY AUDIENCE, AND HARNESS TECHNOLOGY TO CRUSH YOUR PRESENTATION

GRACE LANCASTER

# CONTENTS

# INTRODUCTION

Years ago, I stood on a stage, bright lights casting out over an audience whose faces blurred into a sea of shadows. My heart pounded as if trying to escape my chest, my hands trembled like autumn leaves ready to fall, and my mind raced faster than the words could follow. It was my moment to speak, inspire, and to lead. That day, I learned firsthand the powerful impact of public speaking on personal and professional growth. This profound experience ignited my passion for public speaking and set me on the path to help others discover their voice and confidence.

This book is designed with a specific goal: to help you overcome the fears that silence your voice and to provide you with the ability to captivate any audience. You, the reader, are at the heart of this book. Whether you are a student or a professional or want to improve your public speaking skills, this book is for you. This book addresses common challenges head-on, from managing anxiety and organizing thoughts under pressure to mastering the Q&A session without a hitch.

This book's foundation in psychological insights, real-life anecdotes, and practical, science-backed strategies sets it apart. These elements offer a dynamic and engaging roadmap to mastering public speaking. You will find hands-on exercises and real-world applications that transform theory into practice, ensuring you successfully understand and apply the techniques.

Moreover, we delve into how to effectively use modern tools like Instagram, Facebook, and YouTube to engage virtual audiences through live events and captivating reels. This aspect is central for contemporary speakers who must thrive in physical and digital arenas.

The advice you will find here is actionable and clear. Each chapter builds on the latter, providing you with a comprehensive toolkit that will lead to noticeable improvements in your public speaking skills. I invite you to approach this journey with an open mind and a commitment to practice.

As we embark on this transformative journey together, feel a sense of excitement and anticipation. Mastering the art of public speaking with confidence is an attainable skill that can significantly improve your personal and professional life. Let this book guide you to conquer fear and seize the opportunity to have your voice heard in a world eager to listen.

# CHAPTER ONE

# UNDERSTANDING THE BASICS OF PUBLIC SPEAKING

You are standing alone on stage, under a spotlight, with hundreds of eyes fixed upon you, waiting for you to deliver a message that could inspire, educate, or entertain. This scenario, while exhilarating for some, can be the epitome of fear for many. Did you know that public speaking consistently ranks among the top fears, often surpassing even the fear of death? Yet, it's an essential skill across various contexts—from classrooms to boardrooms—and remains a significant hurdle for countless individuals.

This chapter aims to demystify public speaking, beginning with a core challenge many face: glossophobia, or the fear of public speaking. We'll explore the psychological roots of this fear and provide strategies to overcome it. You'll learn how to harness the power of body language, master vocal variety, and strategically use silence to improve your message. Understanding and addressing these fundamental aspects can unlock your potential to communicate effectively in any public setting.

As we lay this foundation, remember that even the most accomplished speakers once stood where you are now. Their journey to confident public speaking began with the basics we'll cover here.

## 1.1 DECODING GLOSSOPHOBIA: UNDERSTANDING YOUR FEAR

The term 'glossophobia' comes from the Greek 'glōssa,' meaning tongue, and 'Phobos,' meaning fear or dread. It's a term that may not be familiar to everyone, but the sensations it describes are universally recognized: sweaty palms, a racing heart, and a suddenly blank mind. Research suggests that glossophobia is one of the most common phobias, affecting as much as 77% of the population to varying degrees. This fear stems not from speaking but from the worry of being judged, which triggers the body's "fight-or-flight" response. It's an evolutionary function that, while applicable in genuine danger, can be crippling in a modern context like public speaking.

The impact of glossophobia extends beyond uncomfortable moments at the podium. It can significantly impair an individual's ability to perform effectively. Physically, it may manifest as trembling hands, a quavering voice, or even nausea, all of which can detract from the delivery of the speech. Mentally, it can lead to a clouded thought process, memory blocks, or severe anxiety, which can prevent speakers from articulating their thoughts clearly. These manifestations affect the speaker's performance and can alter the audience's reception of the message, potentially undermining the speaker's credibility and communication effectiveness.

Mitigating this fear begins with understanding and strategic intervention. Cognitive-behavioral techniques offer a powerful toolkit for reshaping the negative thought patterns that fuel glossophobia. Cognitive restructuring, for example, focuses on recognizing and confronting negative thought patterns about public speaking, such as anxiety over errors or fear of severe criticism. Speakers can reduce anxiety by systematically replacing these thoughts with more rational, supportive ones. Exposure therapy, another effective method, involves gradually and repeatedly exposing oneself to speaking in front of an audience, which can desensitize the fear response over time. Starting with imagining speaking in front of a crowd and progressively working up to giving speeches in more public settings helps build confidence and reduce anxiety.

Inspiration can also come from those who have conquered their fear of public speaking. Consider the case of Clara, a young woman who went from avoiding public speaking tasks in college to becoming a sought-after corporate trainer. Clara's journey involved joining a public speaking club, where she practiced regularly in a supportive environment, received constructive feedback, and learned to manage her anxiety. Her story is a testament to the fact that it is possible to move beyond glossophobia and become an effective, confident speaker with the right strategies and support.

### *Self-Assessment Quiz*

Take this brief quiz to further understand your relationship with public speaking and identify specific fears. Reflect on your answers to tailor the coping strategies mentioned in this chapter to your needs:

1. Do you avoid situations where you might have to speak in front of others?
2. How anxious do you feel when you think about public speaking?
3. What thoughts typically go through your mind before you begin a speech?
4. Are there physical symptoms that you experience when presenting in public?
5. What is your biggest concern about speaking in front of others?

This quiz aims to pinpoint your fears and trigger points, allowing for a more focused approach to overcoming glossophobia and enhancing your public speaking skills.

## 1.2 THE ROLE OF BODY LANGUAGE: ENHANCING YOUR MESSAGE

Communication is not solely about the words spoken; it is equally about how those words are delivered. Body language is integral to public speaking, often determining how well the audience receives the message. This includes everything from your posture to your gestures and facial expressions. Each element sends a powerful signal to your audience, influencing their perception and engagement with your message.

Posture is foundational. A speaker who stands upright with an open stance projects confidence and readiness to engage with the audience. This posture affects how the audience perceives the speaker and how the speaker feels. Psychological studies suggest that adopting a power pose, even if just for a few minutes before a speech, can increase feelings of confidence and reduce stress. On the other hand, slouching or closing off the body with crossed arms can suggest insecurity or defensiveness, potentially alienating the audience.

Mastering gestures is necessary to elevate your nonverbal communication. Think of them as visual punctuation for your words. When used strategically, they can amplify your message—like using your fingers to count off points and giving your argument a clear, easy-to-follow structure. But beware of overdoing it; constant hand-flapping or fidgeting can derail your audience's focus and cause broadcast anxiety.

Your face is equally powerful. It's the emotional canvas for your speech, painting your attitudes and feelings in real-time. A well-timed smile can warm up the room and draw listeners in. Conversely, maintaining a serious expression might be crucial when tackling weighty subjects, preserving the gravity of your message.

The art lies in synchronizing these physical cues with your content. When your words, gestures, and expressions align, you create a cohesive, compelling presence that reinforces your message on multiple levels.

Here are some practical exercises to improve your body language and gestures:

1. **Mirror Practice:** Stand in front of a mirror and deliver parts of your speech. Watch your gestures and facial expressions. Are they natural? Do they complement your words? Practice until your movements feel fluid and purposeful.

2. **Video Analysis:** Record yourself giving a presentation. Review the footage with the sound off. This helps you focus solely on your nonverbal cues. Look for unconscious habits or distracting movements.

3. **The Pause-and-Pose Exercise:** Randomly pause and hold your position while rehearsing. Is your stance confident? Are your hands in a natural, open position? This will help you become aware of your default body language.

4. **Gesture Variety Drill:** List 5-10 key points from your speech and practice expressing each with a different gesture. This drill expands your nonverbal vocabulary and helps you match gestures to content.

5. **Emotional Expression Practice:** Choose various emotions relevant to your speech (enthusiasm, concern, determination) and practice conveying these through facial expressions and body language without speaking.

6. **The "Hands in Pockets" Challenge:** Deliver part of your speech with your hands in your pockets. Then, do it again using gestures. This highlights the impact of hand movements on your delivery.

7. **Feedback Sessions:** Present to a small group of friends or colleagues. Ask them to focus on your body language and provide specific feedback.

8. **The "Mute Button" Exercise:** Practice your speech focusing solely on nonverbal communication. Can you convey your main points without words?

Understanding and mastering body language is not an overnight achievement but a skill refined over time and practice. It requires a speaker to be fully aware of their body and movements and the subconscious messages these elements send. This awareness, coupled with deliberate practice, can significantly elevate the effectiveness of your public speaking, ensuring that your message resonates with and lingers in the minds of your audience.

## 1.3 VOCAL VARIETY: HOW TO USE YOUR VOICE EFFECTIVELY

Your voice is your most powerful tool as a speaker. It's not just what you say but how you say it that can make or break your presentation. Think of your voice as an instrument - when played skillfully, it can captivate your audience and bring your message to life.

Vocal variety is imperative. It's about strategically changing your pitch, pace, and volume to engage listeners. A flat, monotonous delivery can make your audience sleepy, while a dynamic vocal approach can hold their attention and drive your points home.

Picture your speech as a piece of music. Just as a song uses different notes, rhythms, and dynamics to create emotion, your voice can convey a spectrum of feelings and emphasis. Varying your tone can express excitement, concern, or intrigue. Adjusting your pace - speeding up for urgency or slowing down for emphasis - helps maintain interest. Modulating your volume, from a commanding projection to a strategic whisper, can effectively emphasize vital elements of your message.

Strategic pauses allow your audience time to absorb the information, create suspense, or emphasize a point. Practice inserting pauses at different intervals in your speech and notice how they affect the delivery and reception of your message.

To illustrate the power of vocal variety, let's look at Martin Luther King Jr.'s famous "I Have a Dream" speech. His masterful use of pitch helped emphasize his passionate plea for equality and justice. At the same time, the varied pace and strategic pauses allowed his words to resonate deeply with the audience, creating a lasting impact. Analyzing such speeches can offer valuable insights into effectively using vocal variety to enhance public speaking.

Here are some techniques for vocal variety:

1. **Pitch Variation:** Move between higher and lower pitches to convey different emotions or emphasis. Practice saying the same sentence with different pitch patterns.
2. **Speed Modulation:** Vary your speaking pace. Slow down for important points and speed up for excitement or urgency. Practice alternating between speeds within a single paragraph.

3. **Volume Control:** Strategically shift between louder and softer tones. Whisper for intimacy, increase volume for importance. Practice a gradual volume increase over a sentence or paragraph.

4. **Tone Coloring:** Adjust the emotional quality of your voice. Practice conveying emotions (joy, concern, determination) while saying neutral sentences.

5. **Emphasis Through Stress:** Stress different words in a sentence to change its meaning. Practice emphasizing each word in "I didn't say he stole the money" to see how it alters the message.

Combining pausing and vocal variety exercises:

Take a paragraph from your speech. Mark spots for different types of pauses. Then, note where you'll vary pitch, speed, volume, and tone. Practice delivering it with these variations. Record yourself and analyze the impact.

The secret is to use these techniques naturally and in service of your message, not as gimmicks. Regular practice will help you integrate them smoothly into your speaking style. Remember, a well-modulated voice isn't just pleasant to listen to - it's a powerful tool for persuasion and engagement

## 1.4 THE POWER OF PAUSE: USING SILENCE AS A STRATEGIC TOOL

In public speaking, the power of pause is often underestimated. When used correctly, pausing is not merely a lack of words but a potent tool that gives your message weight. It allows your audience to absorb your points and builds anticipation for what's to come. Understanding and mastering the strategic use of silence can elevate your speaking effectiveness, transforming your presentations into engaging, impactful experiences.

Pauses serve multiple purposes in speech. They allow time for emphasis, allowing your audience to consider essential points more deeply. This can be particularly effective after delivering a key statistic, a provocative question, or a powerful statement, where a pause lets the significance of the words sink in. Pauses play a vital role in audience comprehension. Especially in complex or information-dense presentations, well-timed breaks allow listeners to process and absorb the content, drastically improving understanding and retention. Furthermore, the artful use of silence can create suspense and intrigue, compelling the audience to stay engaged as they anticipate what you will say next.

The technique of integrating pauses naturally into your speech involves mindfulness and practice. Begin by identifying the main points in your speech where pausing could amplify the message or allow for reflection. These are typically moments immediately following a significant statement, before a transition in topic, or after posing a rhetorical question. To ensure pauses feel natural rather than forced, practice your speech and experiment with the timing and length of pauses, adjusting based on the natural rhythm of your delivery and the complexity of the content.

The impact of strategic pause on audience engagement is profound. Psychological studies indicate that well-timed pauses can increase the persuasiveness of a speech and boost a speaker's credibility. From a cognitive perspective, pauses allow the brain processing time, which is essential for effective listening and comprehension. This helps the audience understand and remember the information presented and keeps them mentally engaged as they anticipate and reflect on the speech content. Expert speakers often leverage pauses to emphasize their points and regain the audience's attention, reset the room's energy, and engage listeners on a deeper level.

Here are some practical exercises to help you perfect this skill:

1. **The Pause Insertion Challenge:** Choose a familiar speech or presentation. Mark specific points where you believe a pause would be impactful. Practice delivering the speech, consciously inserting these pauses. Record your performance and listen back. Ask yourself: Do the pauses feel natural? Do they emphasize key points effectively? Adjust the duration and placement of pauses based on your analysis.

2. **The Feedback Loop:** Deliver your speech to a small, trusted audience. Ask them to focus specifically on your use of pauses. Encourage honest feedback: Were the pauses effective? Did they enhance or detract from the message? Were there moments where a pause would have been beneficial but was missing? Use this input to refine your technique.

3. **The Impromptu Pause Practice:** Set a timer for one minute. Choose a random topic and begin speaking. Challenge yourself to incorporate at least three strategic pauses during your impromptu speech. After each attempt, reflect on how the pauses affected your delivery and message clarity. This

exercise builds your ability to use silence effectively, even in unplanned speaking situations.

4. **The Emotional Impact Pause:** Select an emotionally charged piece of text—perhaps a dramatic monologue or a powerful speech. Practice reading it aloud, focusing on using pauses to heighten emotional impact. Experiment with the length and placement of pauses to see how they affect the emotional resonance of the words.

5. **The Pause-for-Emphasis Drill:** Create a list of impactful statements or key points. Practice delivering each statement followed by a deliberate pause. Gradually increase the duration of the pause, noting how it affects the weight and impact of the statement. This helps you gauge the optimal pause length for emphasizing crucial information.

Incorporating these strategies and exercises into your preparation routine will steadily refine your skill in using pauses effectively, making your public speeches more engaging, persuasive, and memorable. Remember, in the symphony of speech, the silences between the notes are just as important as the notes themselves. By mastering the strategic use of pause, you equip yourself with a subtle yet powerful tool that can significantly elevate your public speaking prowess.

# CHAPTER TWO

# PREPARING YOUR MIND AND BODY

Visualize yourself stepping onto a stage, the audience's eyes fixed upon you, their attention on the silence before you speak. Now, picture your heart rate slowing, your breath steady and controlled, a calm washing over you. This is the power of mastering your physiological responses through breathing techniques, a fundamental skill for any public speaker. Did you know that controlled breathing can lower your heart rate and blood pressure in just a few minutes? Envision harnessing this power right before your next big speech. In this chapter, we explore how you can harness the power of breath to transform anxiety into poise and assurance. We'll explore proven breathing techniques, mindfulness practices, strategies for handling physical symptoms, and how your attire can influence your confidence. Mastering these skills will prepare your mind and body to deliver robust, persuasive presentations.

## 2.1 BREATHING TECHNIQUES FOR CALM AND CONTROL

Breathing, an act as natural as it is essential, holds the solution to managing anxiety—not just in public speaking but in any high-stress situation. Controlled breathing exercises can physiologically counteract the body's natural stress responses, such as increased heart rate and rapid breathing, often triggered by adrenaline. By learning to control your breathing, you can directly influence your heart rate, send calming signals to your brain, and shift your body into a more relaxed state.

Let's explore breathing techniques to incorporate into your public speaking routine to stabilize your emotions and maintain composure. One effective method is diaphragmatic breathing, or "belly breathing," which focuses on deep, even breaths that fully engage your diaphragm. Practice this by placing one hand on your chest and the other on your belly; as you breathe in slowly through your nose, your belly should rise more than your chest. This technique enhances oxygen exchange and stimulates the parasympathetic nervous system, promoting a state of calm.

Another powerful technique is the 4-7-8 method, developed by Dr. Andrew Weil. It's straightforward:

- Breathe in through your nose for four seconds.
- Hold your breath for seven seconds.
- Exhale entirely through your mouth for eight seconds.

This method is believed to reduce anxiety and encourage a sense of calm, which is especially beneficial for individuals preparing to speak in public.

Paced breathing is another tool involving the gradual slowing of your breathing rate. Begin by inhaling and exhaling at an average pace, then gradually extend the length of each breath. Aim to lengthen your exhales to be twice as long as your inhales; this helps activate the body's relaxation response.

To maximize the effectiveness of these techniques, integrate them into your pre-speech routine. Start by dedicating a few minutes to breathing exercises before rehearsing your speech. This exercise calms your mind and sets a focused tone for your practice session. Over time, these pre-speech breathing exercises will become a ritual, signaling to your body and mind that it's time to enter a state of calm and focus, readying you for the stage.

The real-world benefits of these breathing techniques are substantial and well-documented. For example, Sarah is a seasoned professional who once struggled with severe anxiety before any public speaking event. By incorporating diaphragmatic breathing into her preparation routine, Sarah was able to reduce her symptoms of anxiety significantly. Her heart rate and blood pressure normalized, allowing her to speak more steadily and confidently. Over time, this practice improved her ability to handle public speaking engagements and enhanced her overall well-being.

This testimonial underscores the transformative potential of mastering breathing techniques. By making controlled breathing a cornerstone of your public speaking preparation, you can confidently empower yourself to face any audience, turning anxiety into an opportunity for mastery and success. As you continue to practice these techniques, they will become an integral part of your skillset, enhancing your ability to deliver compelling, confident presentations that captivate and engage.

## 2.2 MINDFULNESS PRACTICES TO REDUCE PRE-SPEECH ANXIETY

Mindfulness, often visualized as a serene meditation practice, holds profound benefits for public speakers, particularly in managing and reducing anxiety. Mindfulness is the practice of being fully present in the moment, aware of our thoughts, feelings, bodily sensations, and the surrounding environment through a gentle, nurturing lens. In the context of public speaking, mindfulness helps you acknowledge and manage the anxieties and fears that arise without becoming overwhelmed by them. By fostering a calm awareness, you can approach your speeches with clarity and focus, minimizing the distracting rush of nerves.

For public speakers, certain mindfulness practices can be incredibly beneficial. Fundamental mindfulness practice is focused attention, which involves concentrating on a single reference point - your breath, a particular thought, or an object. This practice sharpens your ability to maintain concentration and redirect attention from distracting thoughts, a skill invaluable during speeches when nerves might otherwise cause your focus to waver. Another helpful technique is the body scan, where you mentally traverse through different parts of your body, observing sensations without judgment. This technique can be beneficial before a speech as it releases physical tension and calms your nerves. Mindful listening is another critical practice; it involves fully concentrating on listening to others without preparing your response. This skill sharpens your ability to engage with audience questions and interactions during a speech, fostering a deeper connection and understanding. Integrating these mindfulness practices into your daily routine can deepen your overall mental well-being and improve your readiness for impromptu speaking opportunities. Start small, with a five-minute focused attention exercise each morning, concentrating solely on your breath or the sounds around you. Gradually increase the duration as you become more comfortable with the practice. Incorporate body scans during breaks in your day or immediately before starting a practice speech, which can help identify and relieve tension areas that could affect your speech delivery. Mindful listening can be integrated into everyday conversations, training you to be present and fully engaged, translating into a more dynamic and responsive public speaker.

Numerous studies support mindfulness's effectiveness in reducing performance anxiety. Research published in the journal Psychological Science found that mindfulness meditation could reduce anxiety levels by up to 39%. Experts in cognitive psychology suggest mindfulness enables more rational, less emotional reactions to stressors, which is necessary when facing an audience. This grounding in evidence makes mindfulness not just a theoretical enhancement to your speaking skills but a practical tool proven to aid in real situations.

Imagine a scenario where a speaker, let's call her Lisa, regularly practices mindfulness for two months leading up to a high-stakes conference presentation. Lisa focuses on attention, body scans, and mindful listening daily. By the time she steps onto the stage, these practices have become second nature, allowing her to stay centered and composed, her mind clear and ready to engage with her audience. Even when unexpected questions arise, Lisa listens mindfully, processes the information, and responds thoughtfully and precisely. Her successful delivery directly results from the mindfulness techniques woven seamlessly into her daily routine, highlighting the practical benefits of these practices in a public speaking context.

## 2.3 HANDLING PHYSICAL SYMPTOMS: SWEATING AND TREMBLING

When you stand before an audience, ready to share your insights and stories, it's not just your mind that reacts—your body does, too. Sweating and trembling are among the most common physical symptoms associated with public speaking anxiety. These reactions are deeply rooted in our biology; they originate from the body's instinctual 'fight-or-flight' response to perceived threats. In these moments, adrenaline floods the system, increasing heart rate and blood pressure, leading to excessive sweating and the muscles reacting with tremors. Understanding this physiological basis is the first step in managing these symptoms effectively.

Several practical strategies can be implemented to address and minimize the visibility of these symptoms. First, consider the power of posture. Adopting a strong, stable stance can help control physical shaking and convey confidence to the audience, creating a positive feedback loop that further calms your nerves. Techniques such as grounding your feet firmly on the stage or using a podium for support can stabilize your body and reduce the likelihood of trembling. Furthermore, strategically using hand-held props like a clicker or a pointer can keep jittery hands occupied and disguise tremors.

Another effective method is incorporating movement into your presentation. Walking purposefully across the stage or using gestures can engage your audience and help dissipate the nervous energy that causes shaking. This tactic needs to be balanced, as excessive movement can be distracting. Therefore, rehearsing movement patterns is essential to develop a natural, dynamic expression that magnifies your speech without overshadowing your words.

Combining therapy, medical treatments, and lifestyle modifications can offer substantial relief for those seeking long-term solutions to these physical symptoms. Cognitive-behavioral therapy (CBT) is particularly effective in addressing the root causes of anxiety that trigger physical symptoms. CBT works by helping you identify and challenge irrational thoughts and fears that lead to physical reactions and by teaching coping mechanisms that reduce anxiety. In some cases, medications such as beta-blockers are prescribed to help manage the physical symptoms of stress, such as trembling and rapid heartbeat. However, these should be measured under careful guidance from a healthcare provider.

Lifestyle changes also play a role in managing anxiety symptoms. Regular physical activity, adequate sleep, and a nutritious diet can improve overall physical health and increase resilience to stress. Techniques such as yoga and meditation can also refine your body's ability to relax and withstand stress, reducing the intensity of anxiety symptoms during public speaking.

The stories of individuals who have overcome severe symptoms of public speaking anxiety are both inspiring and instructive. Take Michael, a young lawyer who would sweat profusely and shake uncontrollably during court presentations. By incorporating a regimen of meditation, regular exercise, and CBT, Michael gradually found his symptoms manageable. Over time, he was able to speak in court with minimal anxiety, his confidence bolstered by his ability to control his physical reactions. Another example is Anna, a marketing professional who dreaded conferences due to her visible trembling during speeches. Through beta-blockers and professional coaching to improve her posture and stage movement, she notably reduced her physical symptoms and eventually spoke at events with confidence and poise.

These personal success stories highlight the effectiveness of combining immediate strategies with long-term treatments to manage and reduce the physical symptoms of public speaking anxiety. Whether adopting better posture, utilizing movement, engaging in therapy, or making lifestyle changes, the goal is to empower you to stand before any audience with confidence, not just unburdened by physical symptoms but poised to deliver your message with impact.

## 2.4 DRESS FOR SUCCESS: HOW ATTIRE INFLUENCES CONFIDENCE

The clothes you wear for a public speaking engagement do more than cover; they communicate. Attire is a non-verbal cue that can significantly influence the speaker's confidence and the audience's perception. When you stand before an audience, your clothing is your first statement, even before you've uttered a single word. It sets the tone for your message and can either elevate or undermine your authority and approachability.

The psychological impact of what you wear is profound. Studies in social psychology suggest that attire influences self-perception—a concept known as "enclothed cognition." For instance, wearing a well-fitted suit might project competence and professionalism and make you feel more confident and assertive. Conversely, casual or ill-fitting clothes might make you feel underprepared or uneasy, translating into a less confident presentation. Therefore, choosing attire that looks professional and makes you feel powerful is a decision not to take lightly.

When selecting clothing for a speaking event, incorporate the following guidelines to ensure your attire is appropriate and empowering. First, understand the context of the event —what is the expected dress code? For formal events, traditional business attire such as suits and ties for men or business suits/dresses for women might be appropriate. For more casual talks, perhaps at educational seminars or creative conferences, smart-casual attire might be more suitable. It's essential to balance comfort and formality; clothes that are too tight, loose, or uncomfortable can distract you from delivering your message effectively.

Moreover, the color of your clothing plays an important role in your overall presentation impact. Colors can evoke different emotions; blue can convey trust and stability, making it a good choice for corporate presentations, while brighter colors might be more engaging for creative or informal talks. Additionally, accessories should complement rather than distract, so keep them simple and professional.

Tailoring your attire to match the event's formality, audience expectations, and cultural norms is key to creating the right impression and establishing credibility. For international conferences, research into cultural expectations around dress can be vital. Specific colors or dress styles might be inappropriate or disrespectful in some cultures, which could unintentionally alienate your audience. Understanding these nuances and dressing with cultural sensitivity can help establish respect and rapport with your audience.

The impact of well-chosen attire on public speaking success is evident in various real-world scenarios. A tech entrepreneur, Bridget, experienced a notable increase in audience engagement after transitioning from casual startup wear to a more polished, professional look for investor pitches. Her refined wardrobe bolstered his credibility and self-confidence, contributing to several successful funding rounds. Similarly, a university professor, Joe, saw positive results after adopting a more tailored and authoritative clothing style. Student feedback indicated that his new approach made him appear more knowledgeable and approachable, leading to increased class participation and improved lecture ratings.

These examples highlight the strategic role of attire in public speaking. Your clothing choices should be deliberate, reflecting the occasion and your style while ensuring you feel authentic and confident. Aligning your external presentation with internal confidence significantly boosts the perception and reception of your message, contributing to more effective public speaking.

As we wrap up this chapter on preparing your mind and body for public speaking, remember that the answer to a powerful presentation extends beyond mere content delivery. It encompasses a holistic approach involving controlled breathing, mindfulness practices, management of physical symptoms, and strategic clothing choices. Each element is crucial in building your confidence and capability as a speaker. As you move forward, remember these strategies as integral tools in your public speaking arsenal, setting the stage for a compelling and persuasive delivery that resonates with any audience. In the upcoming chapter, we will delve into organizing your content to allow your prepared mind and body to effectively communicate ideas that resonate and endure.

# CHAPTER THREE

# STRUCTURING YOUR CONTENT

Again, envision yourself on stage. The room falls silent, and all eyes turn to you. Those first few words you speak are your golden ticket to win over your audience or lose them entirely. Did you know that research shows you have just 7 seconds to make a strong first impression? Your opening isn't just a warm-up; it's your best shot at making a real connection.

In this chapter, you'll learn how to create an opener that hooks your listeners. We'll cover techniques to grab attention, set the right mood, and make sure your message sticks. But we won't stop there. You'll discover how to structure your entire speech for maximum impact, from crafting a compelling body to delivering a conclusion that leaves a lasting impression. We'll also explore the art of seamless transitions, ensuring your ideas flow logically and keep your audience engaged throughout.

By the end of this chapter, you'll know how to start your talk with a bang, maintain momentum, and close with power.

Whether you're giving a brief presentation or a keynote address, these structuring techniques will help you deliver your message with clarity and impact, leaving your audience informed, inspired, and eager to hear more.

## 3.1 CRAFTING YOUR OPENING: HOOK YOUR AUDIENCE EARLY

The importance of a strong opening cannot be overstated. It's your first interaction with the audience, and as the adage goes, "You never get a second chance to make a first impression." A compelling start captivates your audience, establishes your credibility, and sets the tone for the rest of your presentation. It should be engaging, relevant, and, most importantly, tailored to spark the interest of your audience.

There is power in a compelling hook. It could be a startling statistic that challenges common perceptions, a powerful quote that encapsulates the essence of your message, an intriguing question that provokes thought, or a brief story that draws the audience into your narrative world. For instance, starting with a statistic like "Did you know that 90% of startups fail within the first year?" immediately highlights a surprising fact relevant to an entrepreneurial audience. Similarly, opening with a quote such as Maya Angelou's "People will forget what you said, people will forget what you did, but people will never forget how you made them feel" can set a reflective and inspirational tone for a leadership conference.

Customizing your opening to fit the demographic and interests of your audience is vital. This customization involves understanding who is in your audience, their expectations, and what kind of message they are likely to respond to. For a room full of young tech enthusiasts, a reference to a recent technological innovation or a story about a Silicon Valley startup might resonate well. For a more mature audience at a medical conference, an anecdote about a breakthrough in patient care or a heartfelt story about a medical discovery could be more engaging. The key is to align your message with your audience's interests, expectations, and emotional tone, making it relevant and compelling to them.

To illustrate a successful speech, let's break down the opening of one of the most famous speeches of the 20th century: John F. Kennedy's inaugural address. Kennedy begins with, "We observe today not a victory of party, but a celebration of freedom—symbolizing an end as well as a beginning—signifying renewal as well as change." This opening is powerful because it immediately sets a tone of unity and forward-looking optimism. By choosing his words carefully, Kennedy acknowledges the historical significance of the moment and invites his audience to contemplate the broader implications of his tenure.

Analyzing such openings can provide valuable lessons in how tone, context, and audience expectations interact to create an impactful beginning. Whether through rhetoric in political speeches, personal anecdotes in motivational talks, or compelling data in academic presentations, the principles of a strong opening remain the same. It must attract attention, stir curiosity, and connect emotionally, paving the way for a persuasive and memorable speech.

As you approach your next public speaking opportunity, take a moment to craft an opening that encapsulates these elements. Here is a practical exercise:

> **Hook Challenge (Crafting Your Opening):** Choose five topics you're familiar with. Create three distinct opening hooks for each topic: a startling statistic, a provocative question, and a brief anecdote. Time yourself, spending up to two minutes crafting each hook. After creating all 15 hooks, analyze which style comes most naturally to you and which seems most effective for each topic.

With each speech, refine your approach and continue learning from your experiences and the examples of accomplished speakers. This ongoing process of adaptation and learning will strengthen your openings and overall effectiveness as a speaker, enabling you to make lasting impressions that inspire and inform.

## 3.2 BUILDING A STRONG BODY OF YOUR SPEECH

Once your opening has captured the audience's attention, the real work begins sustaining that interest and ensuring that your message resonates and remains memorable. This is where the body of your speech plays an essential role. It's the core of your presentation, where you delve into the details, present your arguments, and persuade your audience. Structuring this part of your speech requires a careful balance between clarity, depth of content, and engagement.

Organizing the content of your speech with clarity and impact can greatly enhance its effectiveness. One common method is chronological organization, where you present information in the order in which events occurred. This is particularly useful for topics that involve historical events or processes. Another approach is the problem-solution structure, where you outline a problem and discuss various solutions. This format is engaging because it naturally builds a narrative the audience can follow and aligns well with persuasive speeches. Lastly, the topical organization involves dividing your speech into a series of related but distinct topics. This method works well for complex subjects that require a breakdown into manageable, understandable segments. Each of these structures has its strengths, and the choice depends on the nature of your topic and the objectives of your speech.

Incorporating supporting materials such as statistics, anecdotes, testimonials, and visual aids can significantly bolster the strength and persuasiveness of your speech. Statistics lend credence to your arguments, providing the empirical backbone for your claims. Anecdotes and testimonials, on the other hand, add a personal touch, making your content more relatable and emotionally engaging. Visual aids like slideshows, charts, and videos can help clarify complex information and maintain the audience's attention. However, it's important to ensure that these elements reinforce your message rather than detract from it. Each statistic, story, or visual element should have a clear purpose and directly tie back to your main points.

Mastering the balance between depth and breadth is fundamental in speech construction. You aim to provide substantial content without overwhelming your audience or diluting your core message. Dive deep where it matters most, but know when to pull back. Let's discuss the "iceberg principle" for complex topics - show the tip, but ensure your audience knows there's more beneath the surface. Prioritize content that directly supports your objectives and resonates with your audience's interests and knowledge base. Effective speeches often follow the 80/20 rule: focus 80% of your time on the 20% of information that's most impactful. This approach allows you to explore key points thoroughly while maintaining a cohesive narrative that keeps your audience engaged and informed.

Engagement techniques are essential for keeping the audience interested throughout your speech. Rhetorical questions are an excellent tool for this, as they encourage the audience to think actively about the issues being discussed rather than passively listening. Demonstrations or live examples can also be powerful, especially for technical or abstract topics, as they provide a tangible reference point for the audience. Encouraging audience participation, whether through Q&A sessions, live polls, or interactive exercises, can also increase engagement and make the experience more memorable for the audience. These techniques make the speech more interactive and help reinforce the presented information, increasing the likelihood that the audience will retain and act upon it.

Here is an exercise to help you practice structuring your content.

> **The Reverse Outline (Building a Strong Body):** Take a speech you admire or have written previously. Break it down into its main points, creating a reverse outline. Then, remove the specific content and use this skeleton to build a new speech on a different topic. This exercise helps you understand and replicate effective speech structures.

By structuring your content effectively, using supportive materials wisely, balancing depth with accessibility, and actively engaging your audience, you can transform your speech from a simple presentation of facts into a compelling narrative that informs, persuades, and inspires.

## 3.3 CONCLUSION TECHNIQUES THAT LEAVE A LASTING IMPRESSION

The conclusion of your speech is not merely an ending but a pivotal moment to reinforce your message and leave a lasting impression on your audience. This final part of your presentation is your opportunity to underscore the main points you've communicated and ensure that your message resonates long after you've left the stage. The purpose of a strong conclusion is twofold: to summarize the central ideas you've explored and to motivate your audience to reflect, act, or change their perspective.

Several strategies can be employed to craft a conclusion that effectively anchors your message in the minds of your listeners. One fundamental technique is to summarize the critical points of your speech. This recapitulation helps to reinforce the main ideas and ensures that they are fresh in the audience's mind as they leave. However, this summary must be concise and impactful, focusing only on the core elements of your presentation. Another powerful concluding technique is to end with a solid call to action. This could directly appeal to the audience to take specific steps, engage with a particular issue, or change a behavior. A call to action transforms your conclusion into a launchpad for audience engagement, giving them a clear direction and purpose following your presentation.

Alternatively, finishing your speech with a provocative thought or a poignant quote can be highly effective. This approach leaves the audience with a resonating thought that encourages them to ponder the subject deeply. For example, ending a speech on environmental conservation with the quote, "We do not inherit the earth from our ancestors; we borrow it from our children," evokes a sense of responsibility and urgency, compelling the audience to reflect on their environmental impact more seriously.

While crafting your conclusion, it is also vital to avoid common pitfalls that can undermine its effectiveness. One such mistake is introducing new information in the conclusion, which can confuse the audience and dilute the main message. A conclusion should be a synthesis, not a place to introduce new ideas. Another error is ending the speech abruptly without giving the audience a sense of closure. This can leave listeners feeling unsatisfied and may cause them to miss the significance of the overall message. Additionally, weak statements or overly general remarks can diminish the impact of your conclusion. Your final words should be definitive and robust, reflecting the importance of your message.

To illustrate the impact of well-crafted conclusions, let's review some notable historical examples. Upon his release from prison (1990), Nelson Mandela's speech ends with: "Let freedom reign. The sun shall never set on so glorious a human achievement." This poetic conclusion captures the hope and magnitude of the moment while also looking forward to a brighter future. Similarly, Winston Churchill's "We Shall Fight on the Beaches" speech ends with a powerful resolve: "We shall never surrender." This simple yet emphatic statement effectively encapsulates the defiant and resilient spirit conveyed throughout his address.

Drawing from these examples, you can see how a well-executed conclusion can elevate a speech from good to unforgettable. Remember, your conclusion is your last chance to make an impact. Whether you recap, call to action, or employ another closing technique, ensure it amplifies your message and leaves your audience with a clear sense of purpose or a new perspective.

Here is an exercise to help you practice structuring your content.

**The Last Word Impact (Conclusion Techniques):**
Write five different conclusions for the same speech, each using a different technique: a call to action, a powerful quote, a full-circle reference to your opening, a thought-provoking question, and a summary of key points. Deliver each conclusion to a friend or

record yourself. Reflect on which technique feels most impactful and why.

## 3.4 TRANSITIONS: SEAMLESSLY CONNECTING YOUR IDEAS

Transitions in public speaking are akin to the connective tissue that holds the body of a presentation together, ensuring a smooth flow and guiding your audience through the narrative or argument seamlessly. These elements help maintain a clear communication path and deepen the audience's understanding of the material. With effective transitions, your presentation appears cohesive, clear, and coherent, which can disengage your listeners and dilute the impact of your message.

Grasping the various types of transitions can sharpen your ability to weave them seamlessly into your speeches. Verbal cues are one of the most direct methods to signal transitions. Phrases such as "moving on to," "another example of this is," or "on the other hand" clearly indicate a shift in focus and help the audience follow the progression of your points. Nonverbal cues also play a major role. Changes in your tone, such as altering your pitch or volume, can signal a new section or an important idea. At the same time, pauses can give the audience a moment to digest the information before moving forward. Visual aids, such as slides or charts, can also serve as transitions, visually cueing the audience to a change in topic or reinforcing the connection between points.

Crafting smooth and logical transitions involves more than just inserting transitional phrases at the end of a paragraph; it requires thoughtful consideration of how each part of your speech connects to the next. Start by outlining the major points of your presentation to ensure a logical flow of information. Each transition should build upon what has been said and set the stage for what will come, reinforcing your speech's overall structure. For example, suppose you are discussing the impact of technology on education. In that case, a transition might involve summarizing how technology has changed teaching methods before introducing the next section on technology's role in student assessment.

As we conclude this exploration of transitions, it's essential to reflect on how they integrate into the larger context of your speech. Effective transitions contribute to a seamlessly woven narrative that enhances audience understanding and engagement. They ensure that each part of your presentation supports and builds on the others, which is crucial for conveying complex information and persuading your audience. Remember, a well-structured presentation with smooth transitions can transform a simple speech into a compelling story that captivates and moves your listeners.

Here are some practical exercises for using transitions and comprehensive speech building.

1. **The Transition Bootcamp (Seamlessly Connecting Ideas):** Create a list of 10 random topics. Challenge yourself to deliver a 3-minute impromptu speech, smoothly transitioning between at least five topics. Focus on creating logical connections between seemingly unrelated ideas. This exercise expands your ability to craft seamless transitions on the fly.
2. **The Story Structure Remix:** Take a well-known story (e.g., a fairy tale or popular movie plot) and

restructure it as a persuasive speech. Craft an attention-grabbing opening based on a vital moment in the story, use the plot points as your main speech body, and conclude with the story's moral or lesson as your call to action. This exercise helps you practice all aspects of speech structure while thinking creatively about content organization.

The next chapter will delve into advanced communication techniques that can further refine your speaking skills. From persuasive tactics to the subtle nuances of rhetorical devices, you'll discover tools that can help you craft more impactful and engaging speeches. As you build on the foundation in the previous chapters, keep in context how each element—from the opening hook to the strategic use of transitions—shapes your overall presentation and enhances your effectiveness as a speaker.

# CHAPTER FOUR

# ENGAGING TECHNIQUES FOR ANY AUDIENCE

Imagine captivating an audience not just with facts or persuasive arguments but with a narrative that weaves through the very fabric of human emotion and intellect, making your message not just heard but felt and remembered. Did you know that stories are up to 22 times more memorable than facts? In this chapter, we explore the art of storytelling and other engaging techniques that can transform your speeches from standard information delivery into unforgettable experiences.

We'll explore the science behind storytelling and how it serves as a strategic tool to amplify the effectiveness of your communication. You'll learn how to craft and deliver compelling narratives that make complex information more relatable and improve retention. But we won't stop there. We'll also explore the judicious use of humor to lighten the mood, build rapport, and discover interactive elements that keep your audience involved and invested in your presentation.

Moreover, we'll uncover the secrets of reading and reacting to audience cues, allowing you to adapt your delivery in real-time. By the end of this chapter, you'll have a toolkit of engaging techniques to captivate any audience, whether you're speaking to a small team or a large conference.

## 4.1 STORYTELLING: YOUR MOST POWERFUL TOOL

At the core of storytelling's effectiveness is its ability to tap into human emotions and cognitive processes. Stories have the power to engage listeners not just intellectually but emotionally, promoting a deeper connection with the content. This emotional engagement is critical because it opens the door to greater empathy, trust, and persuasion. Furthermore, narratives can simplify complex information, making it more accessible and relatable for the audience. This is particularly beneficial in technical or data-heavy presentations where presenting direct data or abstract concepts can be challenging for the audience to understand or remember. By embedding these elements within a story, you can create a context that fosters better understanding and recall. Moreover, stories are memorable; they stick in our minds much longer than isolated facts or figures. The narrative format mimics how we naturally think and process information, which helps increase retention and recall.

A compelling story is built around character, conflict, and resolution. These elements serve as the backbone of narrative construction, providing a structure that guides the story's development. The character does not always have to be a person; it can be a company, a community, or even an idea, as long as it allows your audience to forge a connection. Conflict introduces the character's challenges or problems, creating tension and interest. This is the point where the stakes are established, and the audience becomes emotionally engaged in the outcome. The resolution is where the conflict is resolved, providing a satisfying conclusion to the narrative. The resolution must bring clarity and insight, offering a takeaway that aligns with the overall message of your speech.

Incorporating these elements into your presentations demands strategic planning and careful execution. Begin by identifying the message or main idea you want to convey. Then, craft a narrative that embodies these elements in a way that supports your message. To illustrate the significance of innovation in business, you could recount the journey of a startup that initially faced traditional market obstacles yet ultimately thrived by embracing novel strategies. In this story, the startup is the character, the market barriers represent the conflict, and the adoption of innovation is the resolution. This narrative makes your message about innovation more relatable and demonstrates its practical application and benefits.

Adding stories to your speeches effectively requires strategic placement and alignment with your overall content. The placement of a story should augment the flow of the presentation, not disrupt it. Typically, stories can be effectively used at the beginning to hook the audience, in the middle to illustrate a point or add interest after heavier content, or at the end to leave a lasting impression. Ensure that the story is relevant to the main content and reinforces your message rather than distracting from it.

Weave your story strategically within your speech's narrative arc to maximize its impact and relevance. It should be seamlessly woven into the flow of the speech, transitioning smoothly from your other points. If you use a story at the beginning, tie it to the main body of your speech through a transitional statement that sets the stage for your main points. If used in the middle or end, ensure it serves as a practical example of the theory or strategies discussed or as a powerful conclusion that underscores your message.

One can use the example of Steve Jobs' 2005 Stanford Commencement Address to understand the power of storytelling in speeches. In his speech, Jobs shared three personal stories from his life. Each story was crafted around the critical elements of character, conflict, and resolution, and each carried a relevant message to the graduating students. His narrative about being adopted, dropping out of college, and being ousted from Apple before making a triumphant return illustrated his central themes of perseverance, passion, and following one's intuition. These stories made his advice relatable, persuasive, and memorable, leaving a lasting impact on his audience.

Another example is Malala Yousafzai's speech at the United Nations, where she shared her experience of being shot by the Taliban for advocating for girls' education. Her story effectively highlighted the conflict between gender inequality and the fight for education rights, making a powerful call to action for worldwide access to education. Her narrative added depth to her advocacy, making her message resonate globally and inspiring action.

These examples demonstrate how stories can be strategically used in speeches to captivate audiences, clarify complex information, and enhance message retention. As you develop your speeches, draw inspiration from such examples and reflect on integrating personal or illustrative stories to bring your messages to life. Remember, a well-told story can be the most persuasive tool in your public speaking toolkit, transforming your presentations into engaging, impactful experiences that resonate with your audience on a deeper level.

## 4.2 HUMOR: WHEN AND HOW TO USE IT EFFECTIVELY

Applying humor to public speaking can be a double-edged sword; when used appropriately, it can significantly elevate your presentation, making you more relatable and helping to forge a connection with your audience. Humor can break down barriers, lighten the mood, and make complex or uncomfortable topics more approachable. You can increase the audience's engagement and make your message memorable by eliciting laughter or a smile. However, humor must be approached cautiously as it can easily backfire if misjudged, potentially leading to offense or distraction from the main message.

Understanding the types of humor that are appropriate for public speaking is essential. Anecdotes are personal stories that often involve humorous elements; they are effective because they are relatable and add a personal touch to your presentation. Puns, wordplays that exploit the different possible meanings of a word, or the fact that there are words that sound alike but have different meanings can lighten the mood. Still, it should be used sparingly to maintain professionalism. Observational humor, which comments on everyday occurrences relatable to your audience, can be particularly effective as it reflects shared experiences and viewpoints. Assess your audience's makeup and your speech's subject matter to select appropriate comedic elements. Puns may not be suitable for a highly formal international conference but could be perfect for a less formal gathering with a light-hearted mood.

Timing and delivery are critical to effectively integrating humor into your speeches. The timing of a humorous remark can determine its impact. Placing a joke at the beginning of your talk can serve as a great icebreaker, helping to relax both you and the audience. Humor can also be effectively placed after a particularly heavy or complex section of your presentation to provide relief and re-engage the audience's attention. Delivering the humorous content with natural timing and without expecting laughter is vital; let the humor feel like a natural part of the conversation rather than a forced interjection.

It's also important to deliver humor with clarity and confidence. Practice your humorous lines like any other part of your speech to ensure the delivery feels natural and confident. Be mindful of your body language and facial expressions, which can amplify the humor. A well-timed smile or appropriate gesture can amplify the comedic effect, making the humor feel more integrated into your overall presentation.

Analyzing real-life examples of humor in public speaking can provide valuable lessons. Think about a case where a speaker used a humorous anecdote to begin a presentation on workplace efficiency. The story, about a comically ineffi-cient day where everything went wrong, not only made the audience laugh but also perfectly set up the speaker's points about the need for better workplace practices. This effective use of humor helped capture the audience's attention imme-diately and made the serious content more engaging. On the other hand, a scenario where a speaker made a joke that played on cultural stereotypes during a diverse international conference. The joke, intended to be light-hearted, fell flat and caused discomfort among the audience, detracting from the speaker's credibility and the overall effectiveness of the presentation. This example shows how humor can backfire if not carefully tailored to the audience's sensibilities.

These instances highlight the importance of understanding your audience and the context in which you are speaking. They underscore the need for speakers to carefully review what jokes to tell and how and when to say them. When used thoughtfully, humor can be a powerful tool in public speak-ing, enhancing your connection with the audience and making your presentation more enjoyable and impactful. As you refine your public speaking skills, think about how you could incorporate humor to entertain, reinforce your message, and engage your audience more deeply.

## 4.3 INTERACTIVE ELEMENTS TO KEEP THE AUDIENCE INVOLVED

Engaging your audience throughout your presentation is no small feat, particularly in an era of digital distractions constantly vying for attention. One effective way to maintain and even heighten audience engagement is through interactive elements. When integrated thoughtfully into your speeches, these elements can transform passive listeners into active participants, fostering a dynamic interaction that benefits both the speaker and the audience. Let's explore various interactive strategies that can be woven into your presentations, such as Q&A sessions, polls, and direct challenges or questions to the audience.

Interactive techniques, such as Q&A sessions, allow for a two-way dialogue between you and your audience, allowing attendees to clarify points, seek further information, or challenge ideas presented. This keeps the audience engaged and enhances their understanding and retention of the information. Conversely, polls can gauge audience opinions, inject a moment of light interaction, or help you change your speech in real-time based on the audience's response. Direct questions encourage individual reflection or group discussions, breaking the monotony and deepening the audience's connection to the content.

Crafting effective interactive segments demands strategic planning to ensure they fulfill a clear purpose and blend seamlessly into your presentation. Begin by defining the goal of each interactive element. Is it to gather feedback, test understanding, or stimulate critical thinking? Once the objectives are clear, determine the suitable placement within your presentation. Interactive elements generally work well after introducing a main point, allowing the audience to apply or relate to the information immediately. After discussing a new concept, initiating a quick poll to see how many in the audience have used or experienced the idea could provide valuable insights and lead to further discussion.

Incorporating technology can significantly enhance the effectiveness of these interactions. Various tools and applications facilitate real-time polling, audience Q&A, and other interactive features. Platforms like Slido or Poll Everywhere allow audience members to submit questions or responses using smartphones, instantly displaying results on-screen. This modernizes the interaction and simplifies the process of collecting and analyzing audience input, providing a more engaging and streamlined experience.

Balancing these interactive elements with the delivery of your main content is essential. While interaction can markedly improve engagement, it should not overshadow the primary message or disrupt the flow of your presentation. Timing is vital; ensure interactions are spaced well and relevant to the content discussed. Too many interactive segments can lead to fragmentation, diminishing your presentation's overall coherence and impact. Opt for a measured approach by weaving interactions at key moments, enhancing and reinforcing your content rather than distracting from it. Effectively incorporating interactive elements into your speeches enlivens your presentation and converts passive listening into active engagement, making the experience memorable for the audience. As you refine your public speaking skills, reflect on how you might use these techniques to enhance audience interaction, making your presentations informative and engaging.

## 4.4 READING AND REACTING TO AUDIENCE CUES

Recognizing and responding to audience cues is vital to effective public speaking. When you stand before an audience, their reactions—whether through facial expressions, body language, or verbal feedback—serve as a real-time gauge of how your message is being received. Noticing these cues can tell you which parts of your speech are engaging or falling flat, allowing you to adjust dynamically to maintain audience interest and connection.

Observing audience reactions goes beyond simply watching for smiles or nods; it involves a nuanced understanding of nonverbal communication. Leaning forward might suggest interest and engagement, while crossed arms could indicate skepticism or disinterest. Facial expressions can provide immediate feedback on the emotional impact of your speech. Are your listeners frowning in confusion or nodding in agreement? This visual feedback is invaluable as it allows you to gauge the clarity and effectiveness of your delivery. Verbal feedback, while less frequent in formal settings, can provide direct insights into audience reactions. This might come in the form of questions, comments, or even the tone of murmurs and whispers across the room.

Adjusting your speech based on these cues is a skill that can amplify the effectiveness of your delivery. If you notice signs of confusion or lack of understanding, you should slow down your delivery, provide additional explanations, or repeat the main points. Conversely, signs of restlessness or disinterest should prompt you to quicken your pace or move to a more engaging presentation segment. Sometimes, shifting to a different topic or incorporating an impromptu interactive element might be necessary to re-engage your audience. This ability to adapt on the fly helps maintain audience interest and demonstrates your competence and flexibility as a speaker.

Practicing responsiveness to audience cues can be developed through experience and intentional practice. One effective method is to simulate speaking scenarios with peers or mentors and ask for direct feedback on how well you read and respond to their non-verbal signals. Another exercise involves recording your practice sessions and then watching the playback to observe how the 'audience'—which could even be a group of friends or family members—reacts at different points of your speech. Note their expressions and body language. Do you need to modify your delivery? How was the audience's engagement?

These techniques improve your ability to adapt to audience cues and enhance the overall interactive quality of your presentations. By mastering the skill of reading the room, you ensure that your speeches are delivered and truly communicated in a manner that resonates with and captivates your audience. This dynamic interaction transforms a good speaker into a great one, making your presentations informative and engaging.

As we conclude this exploration of engaging techniques for any audience, it's evident that the basis for effective public speaking lies in the dynamic relationship between the speaker and the audience. Each strategy is pivotal in enhancing this connection, from storytelling to humor, from interactive elements to reading audience cues. These techniques enable you to not only deliver your message but to do so in a way that is engaging, responsive, and impactful.

The next chapter will delve deeper into advanced communication skills that can further refine your public speaking prowess. These skills will build on the foundation in the previous chapters, equipping you with sophisticated tools and techniques to elevate your speaking engagements to new heights of effectiveness and influence. As you continue reading, remember that the art of public speaking is a journey of learning, adapting, and evolving—a journey that not only enhances your ability to communicate but also deepens your connection with those you seek to inspire and influence.

# CHAPTER FIVE

# MASTERING PUBLIC SPEAKING IN THE DIGITAL AGE

Did you know that 63% of people find virtual meetings more accessible and convenient than in-person ones? In today's interconnected world, where digital landscapes continually evolve and redefine how we communicate, mastering the art of virtual presentations has become indispensable. Every day, countless webinars, online workshops, and virtual conferences occur across various platforms, offering unique features and tools to enhance digital communication. As you step into this digital arena, whether as a seasoned speaker or a novice, understanding how to leverage these technologies effectively will substantially amplify your ability to engage and influence audiences globally.

This chapter will equip you with the skills to excel in the digital speaking landscape. We'll explore how to choose the right technology for your virtual presentations, ensuring your message isn't lost in technical difficulties. You'll learn innovative strategies for engaging remote audiences, keeping them attentive and involved despite the physical distance. We'll delve into the art of creating compelling visual aids that reinforce rather than distract from your message. Additionally, we'll cover best practices for live streaming on social media platforms, opening new avenues for reaching and interacting with your audience.

By the end of this chapter, you'll be prepared to deliver impactful presentations in any digital format, transforming potential technological barriers into opportunities for connection and influence.

## 5.1 CHOOSING THE RIGHT TECHNOLOGY FOR VIRTUAL PRESENTATIONS

Navigating the myriad of virtual presentation platforms available today can be daunting. Each platform, from Zoom and Microsoft Teams to Google Meet, offers specific features and tools tailored to different interactions and audiences. For example, Zoom is renowned for its reliability and extensive functionality, including breakout rooms for smaller group discussions, a robust polling feature, and customizable backgrounds. On the other hand, Microsoft Teams is integrated deeply with Office 365, making it ideal for presentations requiring seamless access to documents and collaborative tools within the Microsoft ecosystem. Google Meet offers a straightforward, user-friendly interface and effective integration with Google's suite of tools, which is ideal for those already using Google Workspace for document management and collaboration.

Choosing the right platform depends mainly on your specific needs. Give thought to the size of your audience, the level of interaction you aim to foster, and the types of content you will be presenting. For large-scale webinars, a platform with robust audience management tools and stable performance under heavy loads, such as Zoom, might be preferable. Microsoft Teams could be the better choice for team meetings or workshops where collaboration is critical due to its integration with Microsoft Office tools.

The technical setup for a virtual presentation is crucial and encompasses more than just having a stable internet connection. Ensuring the hardware and software components are configured correctly can distinguish between a smooth presentation and one fraught with disruptions. Essential hardware includes a high-quality microphone and camera; clear audio and visuals are paramount to maintaining professionalism and audience engagement. Use an external microphone rather than your built-in microphone for better sound quality. Position your camera at eye level to simulate a face-to-face interaction with your audience.

The software requirements extend beyond the presentation platform. This includes presentation software like PowerPoint or Keynote and possibly additional apps for audience interaction, such as polling software or apps for live Q&A sessions. Ensuring compatibility between these tools and your chosen platform is essential to avoid last-minute hiccups. Some platforms require specific software versions or operate more smoothly on certain operating systems. Familiarize yourself with these details well before your presentation to ensure a seamless experience.

Integrating other tools with your chosen platform can be highly effective in enhancing the interactivity and dynamism of your virtual presentations. Tools like MentiMeter for live polls and quizzes or Trello for real-time project collaboration can improve participant engagement. These tools make the session more interactive and provide valuable feedback and data that can be used to tailor your presentation in real time to meet your audience's needs better.

Setting up these integrations involves linking the tools through APIs or using plugins provided by the platform. Test these integrations thoroughly before the actual presentation to troubleshoot any issues. This preparation ensures that your presentation will run smoothly, allowing you to focus on delivering your content effectively.

Even with thorough preparation, technical issues can arise during virtual presentations. Common problems include audio issues, video lags, or connectivity problems. Preparing to handle these issues smoothly is necessary for maintaining professionalism and minimizing disruption. Always have a contingency plan, such as pre-recorded segments of your presentation that can be played if live streaming fails or having backup devices ready to go. Additionally, familiarize yourself with the troubleshooting guides provided by your platform and conduct a technical rehearsal to anticipate potential problems.

In particular, if your microphone fails during the presentation, quickly switching to an alternative audio source can save valuable time and reduce audience frustration. Similarly, if participants report difficulty viewing your slides, quickly adjusting the display settings or sharing a direct link to the presentation can help maintain the flow of your session.

By choosing the right technology, setting up your equipment correctly, integrating useful tools, and being prepared to handle technical issues, you can master the art of virtual presentations. This mastery enhances your versatility as a speaker and expands your reach, allowing you to connect with audiences no matter where they are. As you navigate the digital age, let these skills empower you to deliver impactful, engaging presentations that resonate across the digital divide.

## 5.2 ENGAGING A REMOTE AUDIENCE: TIPS AND TRICKS

Engaging a remote audience requires combining traditional speaking skills and strategies tailored to digital interactions. Establishing a connection with your audience in a virtual environment is fundamentally about recreating the personal touch of face-to-face interactions within a digital framework. One of the most effective ways to achieve this is through deliberate eye contact, which, in the virtual setting, translates to looking directly into the camera. This simple yet impactful technique helps simulate direct eye contact with your audience, fostering a sense of intimacy and engagement. Similarly, voice modulation is crucial in maintaining audience interest and conveying emotions and enthusiasm. Varied intonations and deliberate pacing help emphasize key points and keep the delivery dynamic, preventing your voice from becoming monotonous. This is particularly important in a virtual context with less pronounced visual cues.

Personal anecdotes are another powerful tool for building rapport. Sharing personal stories or experiences relevant to your topic can make your content more relatable and engaging. These anecdotes illustrate your points and help humanize you as the speaker, breaking down the digital barrier. They can also evoke emotional responses that deepen the audience's connection to the material, making the experience more memorable. When selecting anecdotes, examine those with a universal appeal or are particularly poignant or humorous, as these elements resonate well across diverse audiences.

Interactive strategies are essential in virtual settings, where the risk of distraction increases. Techniques like virtual breakout rooms can be incredibly effective for encouraging participation and making large meetings feel more personal and manageable. These smaller groups allow for more in-depth discussions and can make participants feel more comfortable sharing their thoughts or asking questions. Real-time Q&A sessions are another interactive strategy that can enhance engagement. Encouraging your audience to submit questions throughout the presentation and allocating time to address these inquiries can make the session more interactive and responsive. Utilizing chat functions during your presentation offers continuous interaction and can be particularly useful for immediate feedback or clarifying points on the fly.

Maintaining the attention and energy of your audience throughout a virtual presentation requires deliberate strategies to keep the content dynamic and engaging. Pacing your presentation is vital; if it is too fast, your audience may struggle to keep up; if it is too slow, you risk losing their interest. Aim for a balanced pace that allows for the digestion of information while maintaining a rhythm that keeps the energy up. Regular engagement checks, such as asking for feedback through quick polls or asking rhetorical questions, can help gauge the audience's level of engagement and understanding, allowing you to adjust your pace and content accordingly.

Visuals play a critical role in maintaining audience attention. Well-designed slides, infographics, or video clips can provide visual stimulation and help illustrate complex information, making it easier to understand and retain. However, it's important to ensure that these visuals are directly relevant to the content and add value rather than serving as mere embellishments. Aim for clarity and simplicity in your visual aids, using high-contrast colors for readability and limiting the amount of text per slide to keep the focus on your verbal presentation.

Gathering and incorporating feedback from your virtual audience is crucial for refining your presentation skills and ensuring your content meets the audience's needs. Immediate feedback can be solicited during the presentation through interactive polls or direct questions, providing insights into how well the audience follows and engages with the content. More detailed feedback can be collected through post-event surveys, offering valuable insights into what worked well and what could be improved. This feedback is essential for continuous improvement and can help you tailor your presentations more effectively to meet the needs and expectations of future audiences.

By employing these strategies, you can create a virtual presentation environment that captures and sustains your audience's attention, fostering a dynamic and interactive learning experience. Whether through the strategic use of eye contact, voice modulation, and personal anecdotes to build rapport or through interactive elements and effective pacing to maintain engagement, these techniques are fundamental in adapting your public speaking skills to the demands of the digital age.

## 5.3 CREATING COMPELLING VISUAL AIDS

In the visual-centric era of digital communication, the design and execution of your visual aids can amplify the impact and clarity of your presentations. Whether addressing a virtual conference or conducting a webinar, effectively using visuals can capture and hold your audience's attention, making complex information more digestible and engaging. Let's explore the fundamental principles of visual design and the tools that can help you create striking visual aids.

The cornerstone of robust visual design lies in three basic principles: consistency, simplicity, and emphasis. Consistency in your visuals helps in maintaining a professional and cohesive look. This can be achieved using the same fonts, color schemes, and layout structures throughout your presentation. This uniformity ensures that the audience isn't distracted by varied styles, allowing them to focus more on the presented content. Simplicity is another critical principle; a cluttered slide can overwhelm your audience and dilute the key messages. To achieve simplicity, use minimal text and ample white space, and only include elements that add value to your point. Lastly, emphasis involves highlighting the most crucial parts of your message visually. This could be through bold text, spotlight effects, or strategic placement on the slide to draw the audience's eye to the main information.

Navigating the array of tools available for creating and managing visual aids, you'll find that each has strengths tailored to different presentations. To illustrate, PowerPoint is widely recognized for its robust features that allow detailed control over every aspect of slide design, from animations to custom template creation. It is ideal for traditional presentations where detailed content must be structured clearly and linearly. Prezi offers a more dynamic approach to presentations with its zoomable canvas, making it suitable for presentations that benefit from a more narrative and fluid structure, allowing you to create a visual journey across the canvas. Canva, on the other hand, shines with its user-friendly interface and a vast library of templates and design elements that make it accessible for creating professional-looking designs quickly and efficiently. It is particularly useful for those who need to create visually appealing content regularly but need more graphic design skills.

Integrating multimedia elements like videos, animations, and GIFs can significantly enhance the storytelling aspect of your presentations, bringing your content to life. Videos can be a powerful tool to convey complex information or demonstrate a process straightforwardly and engagingly. Including short, relevant video clips can break up the monotony of a presentation and re-engage audiences. Animations add an element of motion to your slides, drawing attention to key points or helping to illustrate a sequence of steps in a process. GIFs offer a lightweight way to add humor or emphasize emotions without the complexity of video. When incorporating these multimedia elements, it's crucial to ensure they are directly relevant to the content and add meaningful value to your presentation. Moreover, testing these elements beforehand is essential to avoid playback issues during the presentation.

Ensuring that your visual aids are accessible to all audience members, including those with disabilities, is not just a courtesy but a necessity. This inclusivity means designing your slides so that everyone, including people with visual impairments, can understand and engage with your content. Start by choosing font sizes that are large enough to be read easily from a distance, which typically means at least 24 points for text and 32 points for headings. Select color schemes with high contrast between background and text for better readability. Namely, dark text on a light background or light text on a dark background works well.

Additionally, use alt text to describe the images and videos. This practice is crucial for audience members who use screen readers. Another consideration is the logical structuring of your content when read by assistive technologies.

By applying these design principles, utilizing the right tools, enhancing your content with multimedia, and ensuring accessibility, you can create visual aids that complement and improve your presentations. These visually compelling aids can help you communicate more effectively, making your presentation seen and remembered. As you develop your visual communication skills, continue exploring new tools and techniques to help you adapt to the evolving demands of digital presentations, ensuring you remain a compelling communicator in any setting.

## 5.4 LIVE STREAMING BEST PRACTICES FOR SOCIAL MEDIA

Live streaming on social media platforms has emerged as a powerful tool for speakers to reach audiences far beyond traditional venues. Platforms such as Facebook Live, YouTube Live, TikTok, and Instagram Live each offer unique features that cater to different streaming needs and audience demographics. Selecting the right platform for your live-streaming event is crucial and should be guided by who your audience is and what technical features you need to deliver your content effectively.

Facebook Live is exceptionally beneficial for events that engage a broad and diverse audience. Its integration with the larger Facebook ecosystem allows for easy sharing and high visibility, making it an excellent choice for large-scale inter-actions. With its robust infrastructure, YouTube Live is ideal for delivering high-quality video content to large audiences and is particularly well-suited for presentations or lectures that may benefit from higher production values. Instagram Live offers immediacy and intimacy, perfect for more personal or spontaneous sessions, and tends to attract a younger demographic.

Engaging your audience during live sessions is about more than just delivering content; it's about creating an interactive and inclusive environment. Addressing viewer comments in real-time makes the audience feel acknowledged and part of the conversation, enhancing their engagement with the stream. Conducting live polls during the stream can provide instant feedback and keep the audience involved. Strategic use of call-to-action prompts throughout the broadcast can guide viewers to engage further with your content, visit your website, or follow your social media profiles, extending the interaction beyond the live session.

The technical setup for live streaming is foundational to ensuring a professional appearance and smooth presentation delivery. Essential equipment includes a high-quality camera and microphone, significantly affecting the stream's quality and, by extension, audience engagement. Investing in good lighting can also dramatically improve the visual quality of your stream. Secure a fast and stable internet connection to prevent disruptions; wired connections typically offer greater reliability than wireless. Setting up in a quiet, controlled environment can help avoid background noise and distractions, maintaining the professional quality of your stream.

Post-event practices are vital for maximizing the impact of your live-streaming event. Immediately after the event, take the time to review viewer statistics and feedback to evaluate the session's success and identify areas for improvement. Responding to comments and questions not addressed during the live session can help maintain audience engagement and build relationships with viewers. Additionally, repurposing your live content for other platforms—such as creating shorter video segments for social media posts or a comprehensive blog post summarizing the event—can extend the life of your content and reach a wider audience.

These practical exercises will help you apply the concepts discussed in this chapter.

1. **Virtual Room Setup Challenge:** set up your speaking space for a virtual presentation. Create three different setups for your virtual speaking environment (e.g., desk, standing, and sitting area). Take photos of each setup. List the pros and cons for each, considering factors like lighting, background, camera angle, and comfort. Choose the best setup and explain why. Practice a 2-minute introduction in this space, recording yourself to analyze your presence on camera.

2. **Tech Troubleshooting Simulation:** Prepare for potential technical issues during a virtual presentation. List five common technical problems that could occur during a virtual presentation (e.g., audio failure, screen sharing issues). For each problem, write down at least two solutions. Then, simulate these issues with a friend over a video call, practicing addressing them calmly and professionally while keeping your audience engaged.

3. **Engagement Tools Exploration:** Familiarize yourself with various digital engagement tools. Research and try out three different online engagement tools (e.g., polling software, virtual whiteboards, Q&A platforms). Create a short 5-minute presentation incorporating each tool. Deliver this presentation to a small group of friends or family members online, gathering feedback on which tool was most effective and why.

4. **Virtual Body Language Mastery:** Improve non-verbal communication in virtual settings. Record yourself giving a 3-minute presentation on any topic. Watch the recording with the sound off, focusing solely on your body language and facial expressions—note areas for improvement. Re-record the presentation, consciously implementing these improvements. Compare the two versions and reflect on the differences.

5. **Social Media Live Stream Practice:** Prepare for and conduct a live-streaming session. Choose a social media platform that offers live streaming (e.g., Facebook, Instagram, YouTube). Plan a 10-minute live session on a topic you're knowledgeable about. Before going live, outline key points, prepare your setup, and practice addressing viewers by name. Conduct the live stream, then watch the replay. Reflect on what went well and what you could improve for next time.

By carefully selecting the appropriate platform, engaging with your audience interactively, ensuring a professional technical setup, and implementing effective post-event practices, you can leverage live streaming as a potent tool to expand your reach and impact. As we transition from this exploration of digital strategies, remember that the principles of effective public speaking remain constant, whether you are addressing a live audience in a room or viewers across the globe. As we move forward, we'll delve deeper into advanced techniques that can further refine your skills and boost your effectiveness as a speaker in any setting.

# MAKE A DIFFERENCE WITH YOUR REVIEW

## SUBTITLE: UNLOCK THE POWER OF CONFIDENT COMMUNICATION

*"The greatest ability in business is to get along with others and to influence their actions."*

— JOHN HANCOCK

People who communicate effectively live more fulfilling lives, achieve greater success, and inspire others. I'm determined to make it happen if we've got a shot at that during our time together.

To make that happen, I have a question for you...

Would you help someone you've never met overcome their fear of public speaking, even if you never got credit for it?

Who is this person, you ask? They are like you—or, at least, like you used to be—less confident, wanting to make an impact, and needing guidance on how to communicate their ideas effectively.

My mission is to make confident public speaking accessible to everyone. Everything I do stems from that mission, and the only way for me to accomplish that mission is by reaching everyone.

This is where you come in. Most people do, in fact, judge a book by its cover (and its reviews). So, here's my ask on behalf of a struggling aspiring speaker you've never met:

Please help that future speaker by leaving this book a review.

Your gift costs no money and takes less than 60 seconds to make real, but it can change a fellow communicator's life forever. Your review could help...

...one more professional advance in their career.
...one more entrepreneur pitches their ideas confidently.
...one more student delivers a compelling presentation.
...one more leader inspires their team.
...one more dream finds its voice.

To get that 'feel good' feeling and help this person for real, all you have to do is...and it takes less than 60 seconds...

leave a review.

Simply scan the QR code to leave your review:

If you feel good about helping a faceless aspiring speaker, you are my kind of person. Welcome to the club. You're one of us.

I'm even more excited to help you overcome your fears, develop effective communication skills, and become a confident, adaptable public speaker faster than you can possibly imagine. You'll love the strategies and techniques I'll share in the coming chapters.

Thank you from the bottom of my heart. Now, back to our regularly scheduled programming.

- Your biggest fan, Grace Lancaster

PS - Fun fact: If you provide something of value to another person, it makes you more valuable to them. If you'd like goodwill straight from another aspiring speaker - and you believe this book will help them - send it their way.

# CHAPTER SIX

# ADVANCED COMMUNICATION SKILLS

Imagine yourself standing at the podium, the audience hanging on to your every word as you weave through your presentation with the finesse of a skilled craftsman. This is the power of advanced communication skills. Did you know that highly persuasive speakers can influence decision-making in up to 90% of their audience? This chapter delves into persuasive speaking—a vital skill that empowers you to convey your message, sway your audience, win their hearts and minds, and incite them to action.

We'll explore the art of rhetoric, a centuries-old discipline that remains crucial in modern communication. You'll learn to craft arguments that resonate deeply with your audience, using techniques that have swayed nations and moved multitudes. But persuasion isn't just about planned speeches. We'll also tackle the challenge of impromptu speaking, equipping you with strategies to think on your feet and confidently deliver compelling impromptu remarks.

Moreover, we'll address one of the most challenging aspects of public speaking: managing hostile questions and interruptions. You'll discover techniques for maintaining composure and turning potentially difficult situations into opportunities to reinforce your message.

By the end of this chapter, you'll have elevated your speaking craft to new heights. Persuasive speaking goes beyond mere delivery; it's about making your speech an influential force capable of moving people, changing perspectives, and achieving tangible outcomes. Whether presenting to a board of directors, pitching to investors, or addressing a public forum, these advanced skills will set you apart as a speaker of remarkable influence and impact.

## 6.1 PERSUASIVE SPEAKING: TECHNIQUES FOR INFLUENCE

At the heart of persuasive speaking lies the power of credibility. Your ability to establish authority on a topic—what Aristotle called 'ethos'—is essential. It is about more than just your expertise; it's also about how you present yourself, connect with your audience, and the trust you inspire. To build this credibility, start by sharing your qualifications in a way that relates directly to the subject at hand. However, credentials alone aren't enough. Demonstrating a deep understanding through well-researched presentations and providing clear, accurate, and detailed content can significantly increase your perceived expertise. Remember, credibility is also about honesty and transparency. Admitting the limits of your knowledge, when necessary, can paradoxically improve your reliability, as it shows integrity and respect for the truth.

Pathos, or emotional appeal, is your tool to connect with the audience on a human level. Emotions drive action, shape opinions, and forge memories. By tapping into the audience's emotions, you can guide them through a journey that informs and evokes feelings. Storytelling is a powerful method to achieve this. A well-crafted narrative involving real-life scenarios, struggles, and resolutions can make your message resonate deeply. Use vivid language and personal anecdotes to paint pictures, stir emotions, and bring your points to life. In particular, if discussing the impact of clean water projects in developing countries, sharing a poignant story of a specific community or individual can transform abstract statistics into tangible human experiences.

Your arguments must be logical and coherent when using persuasion. This aspect of persuasion, known as logos, involves using reasoned discourse to lead your audience to a logical conclusion. Support your arguments with data, facts, and a clear line of reasoning. Each point should be well-supported and contribute directly to your overall argument. Logically structuring these points ensures your audience can follow along easily. For instance, if arguing for more renewable energy usage, start by presenting the current issues with non-renewable sources, followed by data on the efficiency and benefits of renewables, and conclude with real-world success stories. This structured approach helps the audience understand the "what" and "why."

To heighten your persuasive impact, employ classical rhetorical strategies that have been tested through time. The rule of three, a technique suggesting that a trio of events or charac-ters is more humorous, satisfying, or persuasive, can be used to present your main points. Repetition emphasizes key points and cements them in the minds of your audience. Strategic rhetorical questions that provoke thought rather than elicit answers can engage the audience to consider their perspectives on the topic discussed. These techniques, woven skillfully into your presentation, can significantly amplify the persuasive power of your speech.

Incorporating these elements of persuasive speaking into your presentations transforms them from mere monologues into dynamic, impactful dialogues. As you apply these tech-niques, evaluate each speech as an opportunity to refine and perfect your craft. Your ability to sway audiences will grow through practice and feedback, making each presentation not just a moment of communication but a powerful catalyst for change.

## 6.2 THE ART OF RHETORIC: ELEVATING YOUR SPEECH CRAFT

Rhetoric, the ancient art of persuasion, has been refining how leaders, educators, and influencers communicate for centuries. It involves more than mere fluency; it's about the strategic use of language to move and persuade your audi-ence. The source to mastering this art is understanding and applying rhetorical devices such as anaphora, antithesis, and chiasmus. These devices add stylistic flair to your speeches and reinforce your message in memorable ways. Anaphora, the repetition of a word or phrase at the beginning of succes-sive clauses, creates a rhythm and a sense of urgency, enhancing the emotional appeal of your message. Martin Luther King Jr.'s "I Have a Dream" speech masterfully demonstrates the impact of repetition. The recurring phrase emphasizes his vision of equality and rhythmically engages the audience, drawing them into a shared dream. This technique creates a memorable cadence, reinforcing the central message and unifying listeners through a common refrain.

Antithesis, on the other hand, involves juxtaposing contrasting ideas within a parallel grammatical structure. This clarifies differences and creates a dynamic tension that captivates the listener. Take the case of Neil Armstrong's famous words, "That's one small step for man, one giant leap for mankind," use antithesis to contrast the physical act of stepping with the monumental progress it represented, making the moment much more profound. Chiasmus, where two or more clauses are balanced against each other by reversal of their structures, can surprise and please an audience with its unexpected twist, making the message stick. John F. Kennedy's call to action, "Ask not what your country can do for you—ask what you can do for your country," is a classic example of chiasmus that challenges listeners to rethink their attitude towards national service.

The effectiveness of your speech also significantly depends on your ability to paint vivid pictures and clarify complex ideas through figurative language. Metaphors, similes, and analogies are tools that draw comparisons that can make the unfamiliar familiar or the abstract tangible. By saying, "Inflation is a silent thief," you make an economic concept immediately more graspable by comparing it to a universally understood threat. This illuminates your point and evokes the emotions associated with theft, thus making your audience feel the issue's urgency. Similes, which compare two unlike things using 'like' or 'as,' can add clarity and beauty to your speech, making your content more relatable and your message more impactful.

Crafting a compelling narrative is another critical aspect of rhetoric. Constructing a narrative arc in your speeches can guide your audience through a coherent and persuasive story. This arc typically includes a clear beginning that sets up the context, a middle that presents conflicts or challenges, and an ending that resolves these challenges, leaving your audience enlightened, persuaded, or inspired. Weaving rhetorical elements throughout your narrative enriches its storytelling aspect and ensures that each part of the story underscores and amplifies your main message. Elevate the climax of your narrative by incorporating a well-chosen metaphor. This technique can powerfully underscore your main point, ensuring it leaves a lasting impression on your audience.

To truly grasp the power of rhetoric in enhancing speechcraft, one must analyze speeches that have stood the test of time. Take the speeches of Winston Churchill during World War II, which are replete with rhetorical strategies that rallied a nation under siege. By breaking down such speeches, you can identify rhetorical devices, persuasive arguments' structure, and figurative language implementation. This provides practical models to emulate and deepens your understanding of how these techniques work together to create speeches that are heard, felt, and remembered.

Here is an exercise to practice rhetorical analysis and application.

1. **Select a famous speech:** Choose a renowned speech, such as Churchill's "We Shall Fight on the Beaches," Martin Luther King Jr.'s "I Have a Dream.", or Abraham Lincoln's "The Gettysburg Address."
2. **Identify rhetorical devices:** As you read or listen to the speech, note at least five rhetorical devices used (e.g., anaphora, metaphor, tricolon).
3. **Analyze structure:** Outline the speech's structure, noting how the speaker organizes their arguments and builds to their main points.
4. **Emotional impact:** Highlight phrases or sections that evoke strong emotions. Reflect on how the speaker achieves this impact.
5. **Modern application:** Choose a current topic that fits your expertise. Draft a short speech (2-3 minutes) on this topic, consciously incorporating at least three rhetorical devices you identified in the historic speech.
6. **Deliver and reflect:** Practice delivering your speech, focusing on emulating the power and conviction of the historic orator. Record yourself and reflect on your use of rhetorical devices.

By mastering these rhetorical strategies and integrating them into your public speaking toolkit, you elevate the style and substance of your speeches, making them more persuasive, memorable, and impactful. Whether you are addressing a boardroom, a classroom, or a stadium, the art of rhetoric can empower you to deliver messages that inspire change, provoke thought, and lead action.

## 6.3 IMPROMPTU SPEAKING: THINKING ON YOUR FEET

In public speaking, thinking on your feet and delivering impromptu responses is invaluable. Whether you're fielding unexpected questions during a Q&A or asked to provide your insights at a moment's notice, the skill to articulate your thoughts clearly and promptly can set you apart as a confident and capable communicator. Preparation, while counterintuitive for impromptu scenarios, is crucial. Staying informed about relevant topics in your field ensures you're always in the know. Regularly engaging with current news, industry trends, and scholarly articles helps you build a reservoir of knowledge you can draw upon when needed. Additionally, practicing quick-thinking exercises can increase your ability to formulate thoughts rapidly. Activities like debating a random topic with a friend or trying to outline a speech on an unfamiliar subject within a few minutes can sharpen your mental reflexes and boost your readiness to handle impromptu speaking scenarios.

When suddenly asked to speak, quickly organizing your thoughts is paramount. A simple yet effective structure to rely on is the PREP method: Point, Reason, Example, Point. Start by clearly stating your main point. This sets the direction for your response and provides a clear framework for your audience. Next, give reasons to support your point. This is where your preparation pays off, as you can draw on relevant knowledge and insights to substantiate your argument. Following up with an example solidifies your reason, making your argument concrete and relatable for your audience. Finally, reiterate your main point, ensuring your message is clear and impactful. This structure not only helps in organizing your thoughts swiftly but also in delivering them coherently and persuasively.

To master this technique, immerse yourself in realistic practice scenarios that mirror the unpredictable nature of impromptu speaking.

***Exercise: PREP Method Mastery***

**1. Scenario Bank:** Create a diverse list of 10-15 potential impromptu speaking situations. Include scenarios like:

- Being asked to give an unexpected project update at a team meeting
- Responding to a challenging question during a public Q&A session
- Providing an impromptu toast at a colleague's retirement party
- Addressing a crisis in a press conference

**2. Topic Cards:** Write down various topics or questions related to your field on index cards. These could range from industry trends to specific challenges in your work.

**3. Timed Practice:** Set a timer for 30 seconds. Draw a scenario and a topic card at random. Use the 30 seconds to outline your response using the PREP method quickly:

- Point: State your main idea clearly
- Reason: Provide the rationale behind your point
- Example: Offer a concrete example or evidence
- Point: Restate your main idea to reinforce it

**4. Deliver:** After the 30-second prep, deliver your impromptu speech for 2-3 minutes, adhering to the PREP structure.

**5. Record and Review:** Record these practice sessions using your smartphone. Review your performances, focusing on:

- How well you adhered to the PREP structure
- The clarity and conciseness of your main points
- Your ability to provide relevant examples quickly
- Your overall delivery, including pace and confidence

**6. Peer Feedback:** If possible, practice with a friend or colleague. Take turns providing scenarios and topics to each other and offer constructive feedback on each other's impromptu speeches.

**7. Reflection Journal:** After each practice session, jot down what worked well and areas for improvement. Over time, you'll see patterns emerge, helping you refine your approach.

By regularly engaging in this exercise, you'll become more adept at using the PREP method and build the confidence to handle many impromptu speaking challenges. This structured practice transforms the PREP method from a theoretical concept into a practical, internalized skill, enabling you to respond eloquently and effectively in any unexpected speaking situation.

Maintaining composure under pressure is another critical aspect of successful impromptu speaking. Techniques like mindfulness and visualization can be particularly effective before any speaking engagement to center your thoughts and calm your nerves. This practice can help you maintain clarity and poise, even when faced unexpectedly. Visualization techniques, where you imagine yourself successfully handling impromptu scenarios, can also be beneficial. By visualizing a positive outcome, you build internal confidence, which is crucial when you need to respond spontaneously. These techniques prepare you to manage the stress of sudden speaking requests and improve your speaking performance by fostering a calm and focused demeanor.

By including these strategies in your preparation and practice, you equip yourself with the tools to handle any speaking situation with assurance and agility. Impromptu speaking need not be a feared aspect of public communication. With the right preparation and mindset, it can become an opportunity to showcase your knowledge, quick thinking, and communication skills, further establishing your reputation as a skilled and adaptable speaker.

## 6.4 MANAGING HOSTILE QUESTIONS OR INTERRUPTIONS

Navigating through difficult questions or interruptions during a speech is an inevitable part of public speaking that can test your composure and adaptability. Anticipating these challenges is crucial to maintaining control and turning potentially disruptive moments into opportunities for reinforcing your message and demonstrating your expertise. Begin by thoroughly understanding your content and considering any contentious points that might provoke skepticism or disagreement. This foresight involves not just knowing your topic inside out but also understanding the perspectives and backgrounds of your audience. By doing so, you can predict questions that might arise and prepare balanced, thoughtful responses that address the concerns while reaffirming your points.

When addressing complex topics like climate change, anticipate common skepticism and misconceptions. Prepare evidence-backed responses to objections, such as claims that climate variability is natural. Extend your preparation to include answers for logistical queries about your data sources and the broader applicability of your arguments. This comprehensive preparation enables you to deliver a persuasive presentation, handle interruptions smoothly, and establish credibility as a well-informed speaker.

When faced with hostility, remaining calm and composed is the key to maintaining control. This requires both mental preparation and practical speaking experience. Use neutral language that doesn't provoke further aggression, and keep your responses focused strictly on the topic. Avoid getting defensive; instead, acknowledge the other person's point of view and provide clear information to counter their arguments. If an audience member questions the credibility of your data, calmly explain the source of your data and its relevance rather than dismissing the question outright. This approach not only diffuses tension but also shows that you respect different viewpoints, which can increase your rapport with the audience.

Turning hostility into an opportunity is an advanced skill that can improve your impact as a speaker. When you encounter challenging questions or interruptions, leverage these moments to strengthen your arguments and engage more deeply with your audience. For example, if someone challenges the feasibility of your proposed solutions during a business presentation, use that opportunity to elaborate on the flexibility and adaptability of your strategies, thereby turning a skeptical question into a chance to showcase the robustness of your plan. This not only helps in winning over detractors but also demonstrates your poise and leadership under pressure, traits that are highly admired in professional settings.

Participate in role-play exercises that simulate challenging speaking scenarios to build these skills in a practical, hands-on manner. These exercises can be set up with colleagues or within a public speaking club, where participants can throw unexpected questions or interruptions at you, allowing you to practice your responses in a controlled environment. Such practice prepares you for real-life scenarios and helps reduce anxiety associated with public speaking as you become more accustomed to handling disruptions smoothly.

To effectively implement role-play exercises, create diverse scenarios reflecting different interruptions or hostile questions you might encounter. Each scenario should challenge a different aspect of your response strategy, from maintaining composure and using neutral language to turning hostility into a dialogue opportunity. After each role-play session, solicit feedback from observers or participants on your handling of the situation. Discuss what worked well and what could be improved, focusing on verbal responses and non-verbal cues such as body language and tone. This feedback is invaluable as it provides external perspectives on your performance, offering insights.

By mastering these techniques, you can transform challenging moments during your speeches into opportunities to showcase your expertise and strengthen your connection with your audience. This enriches your presentations and builds your reputation as a confident, capable, and resilient speaker.

As we conclude this exploration of advanced communication skills, we see how effectively handling difficult questions and interruptions is not merely about defending your stance but about engaging constructively with your audience. When navigated skillfully, these challenges can boost your credibility and deepen the impact of your message. The next chapter will focus on specific contexts and audiences, providing tailored strategies for adapting your public speaking skills to meet various situational demands. This shift from general techniques to specific applications will further equip you to deliver compelling, impactful presentations across diverse platforms and audiences.

# CHAPTER SEVEN

# OVERCOMING SPECIFIC CHALLENGES

Do you experience a flutter in your stomach or a quickening of your pulse when you step on the stage? If yes, then you are not alone. Studies have shown up to 75% of people experience some degree of anxiety or nervousness when public speaking. This is when nervous energy peaks, threatening to cloud your thoughts and unsteady your voice. Yet, if channeled correctly, this energy can transform a routine presentation into a riveting performance. This chapter explores the alchemy of turning this nervous energy into a powerful ally—enthusiasm.

We'll delve into proven techniques for harnessing your adrenaline and redirecting it into passionate delivery. However, overcoming challenges in public speaking goes beyond managing nerves. We'll also tackle unforeseen technical issues, equipping you with strategies to handle those dreaded moments when technology fails mid-presentation.

For those expanding their reach globally, we'll explore techniques for speaking confidently in a second language, helping you connect with diverse audiences. Additionally, we'll address the art of handling difficult audience members and turning potential disruptions into opportunities for engagement.

By the end of this chapter, you'll have a toolkit of strategies to overcome specific challenges in public speaking. Whether battling nerves, technical glitches, language barriers, or tough

## 7.1 TURNING NERVOUS ENERGY INTO ENTHUSIASM

Nervous energy in public speaking is a universal phenomenon experienced by novices and seasoned speakers alike. It stems from the body's natural response to perceived threats—the fight-or-flight response—triggering the release of adrenaline and cortisol, which prepares your body for rapid action. Physiologically, this can manifest as a fast heartbeat, sweating, and shaking, symptoms often mistaken for fear. Psychologically, it heightens your senses and sharpens your focus, although when mismanaged, it can lead to overwhelming anxiety.

Understanding this nervous energy's dual nature—it is both an obstacle and an asset—is a solution to transforming it. By reframing the physical symptoms as signs of readiness rather than fear, you can begin to harness this energy effectively. Recognize that the physiological arousal preparing you to 'fight' or 'flee' can energize your delivery, intensify your passion, and engage your audience. This shift in perspective is the first step towards turning nervous energy into enthusiastic expression.

Several techniques can help you convert anxiety into excitement and enthusiasm. Visualization is a powerful tool in this arsenal. Before your presentation, take a moment to close your eyes and imagine yourself delivering your speech confidently. Visualize the audience's positive reactions, the applause, and the sense of accomplishment. This mental rehearsal primes your brain to perform the envisioned actions and transforms anxiety into anticipation.

Positive self-talk is another critical technique. Challenge negative thoughts that arise, such as "I'm going to fail" or "They won't like what I have to say," and replace them with affirmations like "I am prepared and excited to share my knowledge" or "I am here to offer value." This cognitive behavioral approach shifts your mindset from a focus on fear to a focus on opportunity and success.

Anchoring techniques also play a vital role. These involve creating a physical or mental 'anchor'—like a gesture or a mantra—associated with feelings of confidence and calmness. The technique of pressing your fingers together while recalling a moment when you felt particularly confident can evoke the same feelings during your speech. Employing these anchors right before or during your presentation can help maintain your composure and channel your nervous energy into a dynamic delivery.

Role-playing exercises that simulate various speaking scenarios, such as presenting to a hostile audience or in a stressful situation, allow you to practice transforming nervous energy into enthusiasm in a controlled environment. Peer feedback during these exercises can offer valuable insights into the effectiveness of your techniques, such as visualization, positive self-talk, and anchoring.

Real-life examples serve as potent reminders of the effectiveness of these techniques. Michael was a once-timid sales executive who dreaded public speaking. Through persistent application of visualization and positive self-talk, he gradually began to harness his nervous energy to fuel his presentations. His newfound enthusiasm improved his speaking skills and helped him connect more authentically with his audience, leading to increased sales and professional recognition.

Sarah, a young entrepreneur, once struggled with stage fright that held her back from pitching her innovative ideas. But through the power of anchoring techniques, she found a way to transform her nervousness into a source of confidence and charisma. Before each presentation, Sarah would take a moment to close her eyes, take a deep breath, and visualize herself successfully delivering her pitch with clarity and conviction. She would then press her thumb and forefinger together, creating a physical anchor that she could touch during her presentation to remind herself of that feeling of confidence. This simple yet powerful ritual helped Sarah convert her anxious energy into a magnetic presence that captivated her audience. Her pitches became not just informative but engaging and persuasive, leading to vital connections and opportunities for her business. Through the power of anchoring, Sarah not only overcame her stage fright but unlocked her potential as a compelling communicator and leader.

These stories underscore the transformative potential of effectively managed nervous energy. They illustrate that with the right techniques and a shift in perspective, what once may have felt like an impossible challenge can become your greatest asset in public speaking. As you continue to explore and apply these strategies, remember that the energy behind your anxiety can energize, engage, and inspire your audiences, turning every speaking opportunity into a showcase of your enthusiasm and expertise.

## 7.2 DEALING WITH UNFORESEEN TECHNICAL ISSUES

In the digital age, the reliance on technology for public speaking has increased exponentially, making it essential to be adept not only at the delivery of your speech but also at managing the technological tools that support it. However, as with all technology, there is always a risk of failure, and nothing can be more stressful than dealing with a technical glitch in the middle of an important presentation.

The first line of defense against technical failures is thorough preparation. Start by creating a comprehensive checklist of all the technical components you need for your presentation. This list might include your laptop, projector, microphone, and any other electronic device you plan to use. Check all devices before your presentation to ensure they are working correctly. It's also wise to familiarize yourself with the setup at the venue, especially if you are using on-site equipment. Visit the venue beforehand to test the equipment yourself or, at the very least, arrive early on the day of your presentation.

Having backup plans is crucial. Always have alternatives ready for every piece of technology you plan to use. This could mean bringing your equipment as a backup, having your presentation saved on multiple devices (such as a USB drive, your laptop, and in the cloud), and even having a printed copy of your slides. In cases where the presentation is highly reliant on real-time data or internet connectivity, prepare screenshots or static data to use as a fallback. By preparing for the worst, you ensure that you can still deliver a compelling presentation, even if technology fails you.

When a technical glitch occurs, your immediate steps can significantly influence how much it impacts your presentation. First, remain calm and maintain your composure; getting flustered will only compound the problem. Inform your audience of a technical issue and assure them that it will be resolved shortly. This transparency helps manage the audience's expectations and buys you goodwill and time.

While the issue is being addressed, keep the audience engaged. If the problem is with visual aids, shift the focus to an oral narrative of your presentation. If it's an audio issue, use visual aids more heavily. If all tech fails, rely on your prepared, printed materials or notes. To maintain audience engagement while addressing technical issues, incorporate an interactive Q&A segment or share a relevant anecdote, seamlessly shifting focus from the technology to your core message.

Familiarizing yourself with basic troubleshooting techniques for common technical issues can save the day. Learn how to fix common problems with projectors, microphones, and computers. Adjusting a projector's resolution settings or rebooting a system can often resolve many issues. Most modern presentation venues have technical support staff, so knowing how to describe and fix the problem quickly is beneficial. However, in their absence, your ability to address minor issues independently can keep your presentation on track.

Maintaining your composure in the face of technical difficulties helps you think more clearly and positively influences how the audience perceives you. Displaying professionalism under pressure can significantly boost your credibility and authority as a speaker. It shows that you are knowledgeable about your subject matter and adaptable and resourceful in unexpected situations. This resilience can make your presentation memorable for all the right reasons.

By preparing diligently, staying calm, knowing basic troubleshooting, and keeping the audience engaged, you can ensure that technical issues do not negatively impact your presentation. Instead, they become opportunities to showcase your professionalism and ability to perform under pressure.

## 7.3 SPEAKING CONFIDENTIALLY IN A SECOND LANGUAGE

Navigating the complexities of public speaking can be daunting, and when you add the challenge of presenting in a second language, the task can seem even more formidable. However, you can overcome these barriers and deliver compelling speeches in a language that is not your native tongue. Enhancing your language proficiency is the first step toward this goal. Focus on pronunciation, which ensures clarity and understanding. Mispronunciation can lead to confusion and detract from your message, so investing time in practicing the sounds and intonations unique to the language is beneficial. Resources like online pronunciation guides, language learning apps, and speech therapy tools can be invaluable. Additionally, expanding your vocabulary is crucial, not just for fluency but also to express your ideas more precisely. Engage with a wide range of texts—books, articles, and podcasts—that not only increase your vocabulary but also expose you to different styles and contexts of the language.

Beyond words and phrases, mastering idiomatic expressions can significantly refine your linguistic skills in public speaking. Idioms can enrich your speech, making it more engaging and authentic. However, the challenge lies in using them appropriately and understanding their nuances, as improper use can lead to misunderstandings. Tools like idiom dictionaries or language exchange platforms where you can interact with native speakers can be beneficial. These interactions not only aid in learning the practical usage of idioms but also in understanding the cultural contexts in which they are used, which brings us to another pivotal aspect: cultural sensitivity.

Understanding cultural nuances is fundamental when speaking a second language. Every culture has unique values, beliefs, and expectations that can significantly influence how your speech is received. Case in point, humor, personal anecdotes, or how questions are asked can dramatically vary from one culture to another. Misunderstandings arising from cultural differences can alienate your audience or obscure your message. To navigate this, immerse yourself in the cultural context of the language. Participate in cultural workshops, attend events, or watch local media productions.

Being culturally informed enriches your linguistic skills and bolsters your credibility and relatability as a speaker.

Practical exercises and real-world practice are indispensable for non-native speakers looking to build confidence. Joining multilingual speaking clubs or online groups can provide a supportive environment to practice and receive feedback. These platforms often offer a mix of formal and informal interactions, allowing you to refine your skills in various speaking contexts—from delivering structured speeches to engaging in spontaneous dialogues. Additionally, simulating speaking scenarios where you can practice speeches or presentations in your second language. This could be as simple as recording yourself and reviewing the playback to identify areas for improvement or as involved as arranging mock presentations with peers who can provide constructive feedback.

The stories of individuals who have excelled in public speaking in a non-native language serve as powerful motivation. Take, for example, a young entrepreneur from Japan who moved to the United States and used her bilingual ability to facilitate cross-cultural workshops. Despite initial challenges with English, her dedication to improving through relentless practice and cultural immersion led to her being invited as a keynote speaker at international conferences. Another inspirational figure is a Brazilian professor who taught himself English and used it to share his research with a global audience, eventually receiving accolades for his engaging and informative presentations. These stories underscore that with persistence, practice, and a willingness to immerse oneself in another culture, mastering public speaking in a second language is both a possibility and a gateway to new opportunities and broader horizons.

## 7.4 HANDLING DIFFICULT AUDIENCE MEMBERS

Engaging with an audience during a presentation isn't just about delivering your content; it's equally about managing the dynamics of human behavior that manifest in real-time. Among these challenges, difficult audience members are a particularly daunting hurdle for many speakers. These individuals can vary widely in their disruptions: from hecklers who openly challenge or mock the speaker to constant interrupters who don't allow points to be fully articulated or even disengaged attendees who may seem indifferent or distracted, potentially undermining the energy of a session.

Addressing these disruptions requires a blend of tact, strategy, and patience. The first step is maintaining control of the room without escalating the situation. This can be achieved by acknowledging the disruptive behavior in a non-confrontational manner. Let's say someone interrupts; a response like, "I appreciate your enthusiasm, and I'll get to your point shortly, but let's first finish discussing the current topic," can reaffirm your control while validating the audience member's eagerness to contribute. Keep your tone respectful and composed, as getting visibly upset or responding harshly may only escalate the disruption and shift the focus away from your presentation.

Turning challenging interactions into positive exchanges can transform potential detractors into supporters. Engaging with difficult audience members—addressing their concerns, inviting them to elaborate on their points during appropriate times, or even integrating their perspectives into your talk—can neutralize disruptions and enrich the session for everyone. This approach demonstrates your competence in handling divergent views and can improve your credibility as a speaker who values audience input and can adapt dynamically to the flow of discussion.

To prepare for problematic audience behaviors, participate in role-playing exercises with your peers. During the mock presentations, encourage your peers to act out as difficult audience members. After these practice sessions, gather feedback on how you handle the situations. Was your tone appropriate? Did you manage to keep the presentation on track? What could you have done differently? This feedback is crucial as it provides insights that you can use to refine your strategies and improve your confidence in managing challenging audiences.

By understanding common disruptive behaviors and employing strategies to address and manage these effectively, you ensure that your sessions are productive and respectful. Engaging positively with challenging attendees diffuses potential disruptions and enhances your reputation as a skilled and adaptable speaker. As we move forward, the lessons learned here form a robust foundation for exploring further nuances of public speaking, ensuring you are well-prepared to face any situation with confidence and grace.

# CHAPTER EIGHT

# FROM PREPARATION TO PRESENTATION

Stepping onto the stage, the anticipation in the room palpable, each gaze fixed upon you—the moment before a presentation can feel like you're about to conduct an orchestra without a baton. Yet, the most harmonious symphonies begin not at the first note played but within the quiet corners of preparation, where every element is meticulously crafted and aligned. Did you know that studies show that an average of 30-60 minutes of preparation is recommended for every minute of presentation time? Your presentation takes root in the crucible of research and organization, poised to grow into an enlightening and engaging discourse.

This chapter is dedicated to transforming the seeds of your ideas into a structured, persuasive presentation that resonates with your audience and positions you as an authority in your field. We'll explore effective strategies for researching and gathering content, ensuring your message is substantive and relevant. You'll learn techniques for rehearsing that go beyond mere memorization, helping you internalize your content for natural, confident delivery.

We'll also delve into the critical pre-speech review, fine-tuning your mindset to enter the stage with poise and assurance. Finally, we'll focus on those crucial first five minutes of your presentation—the make-or-break moments that set the tone for your speech.

By the end of this chapter, you'll have a comprehensive roadmap for preparation, from the initial concept to the moment you step on stage. You'll understand how to craft a presentation that informs and captivates, leaving your audience eager to hear more.

## 8.1 RESEARCHING AND GATHERING CONTENT EFFECTIVELY

In the digital age, where information is abundant and sources are manifold, the challenge often lies not in finding content but in discerning which content is worthy of inclusion in your presentation. The credibility of your sources directly impacts the integrity of your speech and, by extension, your credibility as a speaker. Start by frequenting libraries, academic databases like JSTOR, and websites known for their rigorous publication standards. Scholarly articles, reputable news outlets, and books published by esteemed publishing houses are gold mines of reliable information.

When evaluating online sources, review the domain: sites ending in .edu, .gov, or .org often denote a higher standard of accountability. Check the author's credentials and publication date to ensure relevance and authority. For emerging topics where peer-reviewed articles may be scarce, supplement with sources from established thought leaders or organizations recognized for their pioneering work. Always cross-verify facts across multiple sources to safeguard against biases or inaccuracies that could undermine your presentation's effectiveness.

With a plethora of information at your disposal, the next step is to organize these insights into a coherent structure that flows logically and supports your speech's objectives. Start by outlining the main points you want to cover. This outline will serve as the skeleton of your presentation, helping you to structure your content in a way that best supports your thesis.

Mind maps are an excellent tool for this phase of preparation; they allow you to visually plot out the relationships between different pieces of information, making it easier to see how best to transition from one point to the next. Each branch of your mind map can represent a different section of your presentation, with sub-branches illustrating supporting arguments and evidence. This method helps structure your content logically and ensures that each piece of information serves a specific purpose in your narrative.

Effective public speaking requires balancing depth and breadth, tailoring your content to your presentation's scope and allotted time, and ensuring meaningful engagement without overwhelming or under-informing your audience. Prioritize depth over breadth for complex topics where understanding hinges on detailed explanations. In contrast, breadth might serve you better when you aim to provide an overview or inspire further research.

Use the "rule of three," a powerful rhetorical device that suggests that information presented in threes is inherently more satisfying and effective. This can be applied to how you structure the presentation—introduce three main points and explore each to a digestible yet insightful degree. This approach ensures that your audience leaves with a clear understanding of your message, equipped with enough context to feel informed but not so much that they feel overwhelmed.

Any information you include should serve your argument by reinforcing your thesis or providing the necessary context to improve understanding. Start by stating your main argument clearly and then use your research to build a case around it. Each piece of evidence should act like a brick in a fortress, fortifying your argument against potential counterarguments.

Strengthen your argument by employing diverse evidence types—statistics, expert quotes, case studies, and analogies— that appeal to various learning preferences and reinforce your points from multiple angles. When advocating for renewable energy solutions, adopt a multi-faceted approach to bolster your position, incorporating various supporting data and perspectives. Statistical data demonstrating efficacy can be bolstered by expert testimonials highlighting long-term benefits. Additionally, incorporating case studies of successful implementations across diverse regions can provide concrete evidence of real-world impact. This comprehensive strategy makes your argument more robust and compelling, as it addresses various aspects of the issue and appeals to your audience's different types of evidence preferences. Remember that your primary goal in preparing your presentation is to inform, persuade, and engage. By meticulously researching, organizing, and presenting your content, you ensure that your speech is informative and a compelling narrative that holds your audience's attention from start to finish. As you proceed, let each fact and figure, each story and statistic, be a stepping stone that builds towards a powerful conclusion, leaving your audience not just educated but inspired.

## 8.2 REHEARSING: TECHNIQUES FOR MEMORY AND DELIVERY

When preparing for a public speech, the rehearsal phase is where the magic of transformation happens—where you turn your carefully crafted words into a living, breathing presentation that can captivate an audience. Effective rehearsal involves more than just repeating your speech; it encompasses techniques for memorizing your content, delivering it naturally and engagingly, and refining it through feedback, all within an environment that simulates the actual conditions of your final presentation.

To ensure your delivery feels both confident and natural, mastering the art of memorization is crucial. One powerful technique is the loci method, an ancient strategy used by Greek and Roman orators. This method involves visualizing a familiar place, such as your home, and associating segments of your speech with specific locations within this space. For example, your introduction might be linked to your front door, your first main point to the living room, etc. This spatial memory technique not only aids in memorization but also helps recall your speech logically and structure.

Another effective technique is chunking, where you break down your speech into manageable, logically connected blocks or chunks. This method reduces cognitive load, making remembering large amounts of information easier. Instead of trying to memorize every word, you can learn the key points of each section and the transitions between them. This not only aids in memorization but also gives you the flexibility to adapt your delivery spontaneously based on audience reactions.

Repetitive practice, while more straightforward, is equally vital. Repeating your speech multiple times helps consolidate your memory of the content. However, to avoid sounding rehearsed, focus on the meaning behind the words with each repetition rather than just the words themselves. This approach helps internalize the content, making your delivery more natural and confident.

Memorizing your speech is only the first step; delivering it effectively is what truly engages your audience. Practice your delivery by paying close attention to pacing, tone, and gestures. Your voice should be modulated to emphasize important points and convey emotions. At the same time, your pace should vary to maintain interest and allow for pauses that give the audience time to absorb information.

Gestures, too, play a critical role in communication. They should appear natural and align with what you are saying, enhancing the impact of your words. Practice in front of a mirror or record yourself to observe and adjust your body language. This helps make your gestures more effective but also aids in maintaining an open posture, which is crucial for appearing approachable and confident.

Feedback from peers or mentors is invaluable as it provides an external perspective on your performance. Organize rehearsal sessions where you can present your speech to a small audience that can give constructive criticism. Encourage them to focus on all aspects of your presentation —from the content and clarity of your arguments to your delivery and body language.

Take notes on the feedback. Use this input to refine your speech, addressing areas needing clarification or where your delivery might fall flat. This iterative process of presentation and feedback is essential for honing your content and delivery skills.

To truly prepare for the day of your speech, try to replicate the speaking environment as closely as possible during your rehearsals. If you will be using a microphone or other audio-visual aids, practice with similar equipment to get comfortable with the technology. Visit the venue beforehand to get a feel for the space. Familiarize yourself with the layout, practice using the stage, and understand the room's acoustics.

If you cannot access the venue, create a similar setup in a different space. Arrange chairs to mimic the seating arrangement, use a similar lighting setup, and practice entering and exiting the stage. This will help you get comfortable with the physical space and reduce anxiety, as the environment will feel more familiar on the day of your speech.

Integrating these techniques into your rehearsal process transforms your preparation into a dynamic practice session that builds your confidence by increasing your ability to deliver a powerful, memorable presentation. Through meticulous memorization, thoughtful delivery practice, constructive feedback, and environment simulation, you equip yourself to step onto the stage to speak, engage, inspire, and leave a lasting impression on your audience.

## 8.3 THE FINAL CHECK: PRE-SPEECH REVIEW AND MINDSET

As the countdown to your presentation ticks closer, the final review phase becomes crucial, a period where precision meets preparedness to ensure flawless delivery. Think of this phase as the final dressing rehearsal of a Broadway show; every part, from the curtains to the costumes, needs meticulous attention to detail. Begin by creating a comprehensive checklist that covers every aspect of your speech. This checklist should include reviewing your speech's content for accuracy and relevance and ensuring that all your data, quotes, and references are up to date and correctly cited. Also, examine the structure of your presentation; make sure there is a logical flow between sections, smooth transitions, and the overall framework effectively supports your objectives.

Materials, too, demand scrutiny. Double-check your visuals, slides, and multimedia components for technical correctness and aesthetic harmony. Ensure that text is readable, images are clear, and that any media adds value to your presentation rather than serving as mere decoration. If you're using handouts, review them for consistency with your presentation content and arrange them neatly for easy distribution. This meticulous review polishes your presentation and fortifies your confidence, knowing that every element is aligned and functioning as intended.

Equally important to your material and content preparedness is your mental readiness. Cultivating a positive mindset before stepping onto the stage can profoundly impact your performance. Techniques like visualization, where you mentally rehearse your success, are effective. Picture yourself delivering your presentation with confidence and poise, receiving engaged nods and smiles from your audience. This mental imagery primes your subconscious for positive outcomes, boosting your confidence. Affirmations also support you; phrases like "I am prepared and capable" or "I am here to share valuable insights" can reinforce your self-assurance and dispel doubts.

Additionally, engage in strategic relaxation exercises to mitigate any bubbling anxiety. Techniques include deep breathing, progressive muscle relaxation, or a brief meditative session. These methods help center your thoughts and calm your nerves, ensuring you approach the podium comfortably.

Handling last-minute nerves is another aspect of your pre-speech preparation. Despite thorough rehearsals, it's common to feel a surge of adrenaline as your moment in the spotlight approaches. To manage this, focus on controlled breathing techniques. Slow, deep breaths can decrease your heart rate and ease the tension, helping you maintain a calm demeanor. Pair this with brief physical exercises like neck rolls or shoulder shrugs to release accumulated stress. These simple physical movements can prevent stiffness and maintain energy levels, keeping you dynamic and alert.

Finally, thorough equipment and setup verification is indispensable. Conduct a final run-through with all your technical equipment to ensure everything functions seamlessly. Check that your microphone, projector, and other electronics are set up correctly and without glitches. If you're using a platform or software for your presentation, log in early to troubleshoot any potential issues with connectivity or accessibility. This proactive approach helps avert technical mishaps and provides peace of mind, allowing you to focus entirely on delivering an impactful presentation.

By meticulously attending to these final details, you empower yourself to deliver a presentation and an experience that resonates with your audience. Ensuring that your content, materials, and mindset are finely tuned and harmoniously aligned sets the stage for a presentation that is not only successful but memorable.

## 8.4 THE FIRST FIVE MINUTES: SETTING THE TONE

The initial moments of any presentation are pivotal; they set the stage for the rapport you will establish with your audience and can significantly influence the overall impact of your speech. A powerful opening not only captivates your audience but also sets the tone for the message you intend to deliver. Imagine opening your talk with a startling statistic, a provocative question, or a compelling anecdote. Starting with "Did you know that less than 10% of people feel confident about public speaking?" immediately grabs attention by connecting with a common fear, setting the stage for a discussion on overcoming this challenge. Alternatively, opening with a personal story highlighting a struggle and eventual triumph related to your topic can capture attention and make the theme relatable and engaging from the outset.

Establishing credibility and building rapport are your next critical steps. This phase is about connecting with your audience in a way that goes beyond the superficial. One effective method is to share a relevant personal or professional experience that aligns with the interests or challenges of your audience. This approach showcases your expertise and demonstrates empathy and understanding of the audience's needs. Displaying genuine enthusiasm for the subject matter is equally important; it communicates passion and authenticity, making the audience more receptive to your message. Remember, your energy can set the energy level for the entire presentation.

Previewing the structure of your talk within the first few minutes provides your audience with a roadmap of what to expect, which helps maintain their attention throughout the session. Clearly outline the main points you will cover and how you intend to transition from one topic to the next. This keeps your audience engaged and helps them follow your narrative more effectively. Say, "Today, we will explore three key strategies to improve public speaking, starting with understanding the fear it invokes, then mastering the art of storytelling, and concluding with practical tips for effective speech delivery," which gives your audience clear markers to track through your presentation.

Engaging your audience from the start can also be achieved through interactive techniques. Asking rhetorical questions encourages listeners to think actively about the subject, increasing their engagement. Involving them through quick polls or showing hands can be highly effective, especially in large settings. Additionally, addressing audience members by name can make the interaction more personal and boost engagement. These tactics draw your audience in and keep them mentally invested in your presentation.

By strategically crafting your opening, establishing rapport, previewing your speech structure, and actively engaging your audience, you set a dynamic tone for your presentation. These first five minutes capture attention, build connections, and set the stage for successfully delivering your main message.

As we wrap up this discussion on the pivotal first five minutes of a presentation, it's clear that the foundation you lay here is instrumental in defining the trajectory of your entire speech. By engaging your audience from the outset, you capture their interest and set the tone for a receptive and interactive session. This chapter has equipped you with strategies to craft compelling openings, establish immediate credibility, and outline your presentation in a way that keeps your audience anchored to your message.

# CHAPTER NINE

# CULTIVATING LONG-TERM PUBLIC SPEAKING SUCCESS

Research shows that speakers who share personal stories are perceived as 4.5 times more authentic by their listeners. Imagine stepping into a room where every ear is attuned to your voice; every eye mirrors the passion in your words. This scenario illustrates the power of authenticity in public speaking—a force that captivates audiences and forges lasting connections. This chapter explores the essence of authenticity, revealing how your genuine self becomes your most powerful asset on stage.

We'll uncover strategies to discover and refine your unique speaking style, ensuring consistency across various platforms and understanding how authenticity improves audience engagement. But cultivating long-term public speaking success goes beyond authenticity alone. We'll explore proven strategies for building lasting confidence, helping you approach each speaking opportunity with poise and assurance.

Moreover, we'll examine how to leverage your public speaking skills for career advancement, turning each presentation into a stepping stone toward your professional goals. You'll learn how to create a portfolio of your best speeches, a powerful tool for showcasing your expertise and securing future speaking engagements.

By the end of this chapter, you'll have a roadmap for becoming a better speaker and building a sustainable, rewarding journey in public speaking. Whether you aim to become a sought-after keynote speaker, advance in your current career, or want to make a lasting impact with your words, these long-term strategies will set you on the path to enduring success.

## 9.1 DEVELOPING A PERSONAL STYLE: AUTHENTICITY IN SPEAKING

Authenticity in public speaking is about expressing your true self through your words and delivery. It's about stripping away the facades and embracing your vulnerabilities, quirks, and individuality. Why does this resonate with audiences? Authenticity fosters trust. When you speak from a place of authenticity, you present yourself as reliable and believable. This genuineness is appealing because it's rare; in a world rife with scripted speeches and rehearsed personas, a speaker who can connect genuinely with the audience becomes a beacon of relatability.

But authenticity goes beyond being authentic; it's about consistency in being true to your character and values, regardless of the setting. Whether you're addressing a boardroom, an auditorium, or a virtual crowd across continents, the authenticity of your presentation should remain the same. This consistency reassures your audience of your dependability and strengthens your rapport with them, enhancing the overall impact of your communication.

Discovering and refining your unique voice is a journey into self-exploration. It begins with understanding the elements of your personality and experiences that shape your perspective and message. Engage in exercises that prompt introspection. Reflect on moments when you felt most passionate and alive—what were you doing? Who were you speaking to? What topics stirred your enthusiasm? Journal these experiences and look for patterns that reveal your core interests and strengths.

As mentioned in previous chapters, recording your presentation helps you determine moments in your speech that feel fluid and genuine. These are clues to your natural style. Experiment with different tones, tempos, and techniques to see what feels most comfortable and aligns with your message. This process is not about crafting a persona but rather about stripping back layers to reveal the speaker you naturally are.

Maintaining a consistent speaking style across various platforms becomes necessary as the world of communication evolves. Whether you deliver a keynote in person, host a webinar, or engage with followers on social media, your authentic voice should seamlessly transition across these mediums. This means your delivery can adapt to different formats; however, your message's core and personal touch should remain identifiable.

Adapt your approach by recognizing and leveraging each platform's unique features and audience expectations. Virtual presentations require a more expressive tone to compensate for the lack of physical presence. Conversely, live speaking may afford more opportunities for interactive dialogue, allowing your natural responsiveness to shine. Practice across these platforms regularly to refine how your authenticity translates in each context, ensuring your style is adaptable and consistent.

Authenticity does more than enhance your presentation; it transforms it into a conduit for deep connection. When audiences see a knowledgeable, genuinely passionate, and honest speaker, it creates a magnetic pull, drawing them into the woven narrative. This connection is potent—it turns passive listeners into active participants, emotionally invested in your words and more receptive to your message.

Moreover, authenticity can significantly boost your credibility. Audiences are perceptive; they can sense incongruence between what is said and the speaker's demeanor. You eliminate dissonance by aligning your true self with your speech, presenting a unified, credible persona.

Incorporating authenticity into your public speaking does not just elevate your presentation; it transforms it into an experience that resonates with your audience, making your message heard and felt. As you continue to nurture and express your genuine self through your speeches, you deepen your connection with listeners while solidifying your reputation as a reliable and relatable speaker. This chapter guides you in embracing and cultivating authenticity, ensuring that each word you speak rings true to you and in the hearts of those you aim to inspire.

## 9.2 LONG-TERM STRATEGIES FOR CONFIDENCE BUILDING

Building confidence in public speaking is akin to cultivating a garden; it requires patience, consistent effort, and the right strategies to thrive. One of the foundational steps in this process is setting realistic, achievable goals. Envision your public speaking journey as a series of stepping stones, each representing a specific, measurable, and attainable goal. For instance, if improving diction is your target, set a goal to practice enunciation exercises for fifteen minutes daily, using tongue twisters or reading aloud. Similarly, if mastering body language is your focus, you might set a goal to record yourself once a week, observing and adjusting your gestures and posture. These goals should challenge you yet be within reach, so achieving them fuels your confidence and motivates you to tackle more complex challenges.

The path to becoming a proficient speaker also involves continuous learning and development. The communication landscape is ever-evolving, with new techniques, platforms, and audience expectations emerging regularly. Staying abreast of these changes is vital. Engage actively in learning by attending workshops, enrolling in courses, and consuming the latest books and articles on public speaking and communication. These educational activities will increase your skills and deepen your understanding of what makes effective communication, from crafting compelling narratives to engaging diverse audiences. This ongoing commitment to learning keeps your skills fresh and relevant, which is essential for maintaining confidence in your ability to deliver impactful speeches.

Regular practice and exposure are equally critical to building and maintaining public speaking confidence. Seek opportunities to speak in various settings, from informal groups like local clubs or discussion panels to more formal environments like conferences or large events. Each platform offers unique challenges and learning opportunities. Speaking at a local meet-up can sharpen your ability to interact intimately with an audience, while presenting at a conference develops your skills in managing larger crowds and utilizing advanced audio-visual aids. Embrace these opportunities as each speech helps you refine your delivery and adapt to different audiences, which is invaluable for building confidence.

Lastly, feedback is a powerful way to foster your growth in public speaking skills. Constructive criticism from peers, mentors, or audience members provides you with perspectives outside your own, highlighting areas for improvement that you might not have noticed. Develop a systematic approach to soliciting and integrating this feedback. After each speaking engagement, ask specific questions that elicit valuable insights, such as "Did the message come across clearly?" or "How could I improve my engagement with the audience?" Take this feedback seriously, but not personally, and use it as a tool to refine your techniques and strategies. Regularly applying the insights gained from feedback ensures continuous improvement and helps solidify your confidence, knowing that you are actively enhancing your public speaking prowess.

Each of these strategies—goal setting, continuous learning, regular practice, and feedback utilization—plays a crucial role in building a solid foundation of confidence in public speaking. By embracing these practices, you ensure that your growth as a speaker is progressive and grounded, enabling you to handle any speaking challenge with poise and assurance.

## 9.3 LEVERAGING PUBLIC SPEAKING FOR CAREER ADVANCEMENT

Public speaking opens doors to numerous professional opportunities, enhancing visibility and credibility within your field. When you articulate your ideas effectively in front of an audience, you do more than share information; you showcase your expertise and capacity as a leader and thinker. This visibility is crucial in professional settings where standing out can lead to career advancement. One strategy to maximize this potential is actively seeking speaking opportunities within your workplace or professional organizations. Volunteer to present at team meetings, lead workshops, or speak at industry conferences. Each platform is a stage to demonstrate your knowledge and skills, positioning you as a proactive and valuable professional community member.

Beyond the workplace, participate in public speaking at community events or through platforms like TEDx talks. These opportunities broaden your reach and enhance your professional profile among a wider audience. By strategically choosing topics that align with your career goals and areas of expertise, you can craft presentations that engage your audience and build your reputation as an expert in your field.

Networking is another significant element in leveraging the public in your career. Effective networking isn't just about exchanging business cards; it's about creating meaningful connections that can lead to professional opportunities. Use your speaking engagements as a chance to interact with your audience before and after your presentation. Approach these interactions to learn about others' interests and challenges and share insights that could benefit them. This proactive engagement demonstrates your commitment to providing value, enhancing memorability, and increasing your prospects for future opportunities.

Furthermore, leverage each speaking engagement as a potential networking hub, expanding your professional connections and opportunities. Before the event, engage with other speakers and attendees through social media or professional networking sites like LinkedIn. This pre-engagement can make your actual interactions more meaningful. After your presentation, follow up with individuals interested in your talk, offering further resources or a one-on-one discussion. This follow-up is a crucial step in transforming casual connections into professional relationships.

Regarding showcasing your expertise, there's no platform more powerful than the stage. Each presentation you deliver is an opportunity to demonstrate your depth of knowledge, analytical capabilities, and ability to convey complex information in an accessible manner. To maximize this aspect, focus on tailoring your content to highlight the unique perspectives and skills you bring to your field. Use case studies, original research, or detailed analysis to provide substantial content that can elevate your professional stature.

Lastly, the ability to convert speaking engagements into tangible career advancements should not be underestimated. After a successful presentation, capitalize on the momentum to further your professional goals and expand your influence. If your talk was well-received, contact your professional network and share highlights or a video of your speech. This can lead to further speaking opportunities or even job offers. Additionally, be proactive in asking for referrals or introductions from your network, which can open doors to new career possibilities.

Incorporating these strategies into your approach to the public can transform your career trajectory. By enhancing your visibility, networking smartly, showcasing your expertise, and actively seeking opportunities to translate speaking engagements into professional growth, you set the stage for a flourishing career bolstered by your skills as a compelling speaker. Each speech, connection, and audience interaction leads you to becoming a better speaker and achieving your broader professional ambitions.

## 9.4 CREATING A PORTFOLIO OF YOUR BEST SPEECHES

In professional development, a well-maintained portfolio of your best speeches can be a powerful tool, showcasing your expertise and the evolution of your speaking skills. Think of this portfolio as a vivid narrative of your journey in public speaking, each speech a chapter highlighting a specific skill, audience engagement, or a unique challenge you've navigated. The benefits of maintaining such a curated collection are manifold. It provides tangible proof of your abilities to potential clients or employers and serves as a personal repository from which you can draw insights for future performances. As you accumulate recordings of your speeches, you'll have the invaluable opportunity to reflect on your growth, note improvements, and identify areas that still need refinement.

When selecting speeches to include in your portfolio, variety and impact should guide your choices. Begin by showcasing a diverse range of topics in your portfolio, highlighting your versatility and breadth of knowledge. Include speeches delivered to various audience sizes and compositions—from intimate workshops to large-scale conferences—to demonstrate your adaptability in message and delivery across different settings. Also, pay attention to the feedback received post-presentation. Including speeches that generated significant positive feedback or led to notable outcomes, such as policy changes, increased awareness, or successful fundraising, can highlight your effectiveness as a speaker.

Your portfolio's electronic compilation and systematic organization are essential in today's digital landscape. Begin by converting all your speech recordings into digital formats, ensuring they are high quality. This process not only preserves your work but also makes it easily accessible. You can use various tools and software to edit these files to improve their quality and trim unnecessary parts, focusing on key moments of your presentations. Effectively organizing these files is just as important as collecting them. Create a digital library where each speech is tagged with relevant keywords such as the topic, audience type, and date. Platforms like LinkedIn allow you to showcase these videos directly on your profile, making them part of your professional narrative and visible to employers, peers, and potential collaborators.

Furthermore, your speech portfolio can be an excellent marketing tool for personal branding. Each speech is a testament to your speaking prowess and demonstrates your professional growth. Share highlights from your portfolio on social media platforms, especially those tailored to professional networking. This reinforces your visibility and engages your network by showing them your active role in your field. During networking events, having a well-prepared digital portfolio allows you to instantly share your work with potential collaborators or mentors, creating immediate feedback and engagement opportunities. Also, when pitching for speaking engagements or consulting opportunities, tailor your portfolio to suit the interests of the committee or individual you are addressing. Highlight speeches that align closely with their goals or needs, making a compelling case for your candidacy.

As we wrap up this exploration of creating and leveraging a speech portfolio, it's clear that this resource is invaluable not merely as a record of past achievements but as a catalyst for future opportunities. By meticulously selecting, digitizing, and organizing your best work, you set the stage for continued professional growth and networking. Each speech, carefully chosen for its impact and relevance, builds a narrative of your development and adaptability as a speaker.

As you move forward, let this portfolio serve as a tool for reflection and as a beacon that guides your path in the ever-evolving landscape of public speaking. The next chapter will explore advanced techniques and strategies enabling you to remain at the forefront of this dynamic field. Let the lessons from your past performances, encapsulated in your portfolio, inform and inspire your journey as you grow, engage, and inspire through public speaking.

# CHAPTER TEN

# SPECIAL CONTEXTS AND AUDIENCES

Envision yourself addressing a room where each listener hears your words through the lens of their unique cultural background. In this global arena, the impact of your speech hinges not just on the eloquence of your words but on your deep understanding of diverse cultural landscapes and your ability to navigate the nuances of global communication. Did you know that over 70% of international business ventures fail due to cultural misunderstandings? This chapter delves into the art of adjusting your speech for international audiences, a skill that demands sensitivity, adaptability, and awareness of the worldwide mosaic of cultures and languages.

But speaking across cultural boundaries is just one facet of mastering diverse contexts. We'll explore how to tailor your approach for educational settings where engagement and clarity are paramount. You'll learn strategies for corporate speeches, discover how to effectively communicate with stakeholders, and drive business outcomes through your words.

We'll also uncover the nuances of public speaking for social events and ceremonies, where your words might mark milestones or celebrate shared experiences. From weddings to graduations, you'll learn how to craft speeches that resonate deeply personally.

As the world becomes increasingly interconnected, your ability to effectively communicate across cultural lines and in various settings can transform a standard presentation into an impactful, context-appropriate dialogue. By the end of this chapter, you'll have the tools to adapt your speaking style to any audience or occasion, ensuring your message always hits its mark.

## 10.1 ADJUSTING YOUR SPEECH FOR INTERNATIONAL AUDIENCES

In international communication, cultural sensitivity is not just beneficial but imperative. Each culture carries values, norms, and communication styles that can dramatically influence how your message is received. Misunderstandings can arise from language barriers and cultural nuances that take time to be apparent. For instance, a gesture as simple as maintaining eye contact is polite and attentive in many Western cultures. However, it might be perceived as disrespectful in certain Asian cultures where indirect eye contact is more appropriate.

Thorough research and consultation with cultural experts are essential to navigate this complex terrain. Talk with local consultants or colleagues who understand the cultural context and can provide insights into the dos and don'ts. This preparation goes beyond preventing faux pas; it's about forging genuine connections. By demonstrating respect and understanding of the audience's culture, you not only improve the receptivity of your message but also build a foundation of trust and respect that can lead to more meaningful interactions and partnerships.

When presenting to an international audience, language differences can impact the clarity of your message. To ensure your message is understandable and impactful, simplify your language. Avoid idioms, colloquialisms, and complex jargon that may not translate well or could lead to confusion. Instead, use clear, straightforward language that conveys your message unambiguously.

When confronting significant language barriers, explore using professional translators or offer multilingual support, such as translated slides or interpretation services, to ensure effective communication across linguistic divides. This not only aids in better understanding but also demonstrates inclusivity and respect for your audience's linguistic diversity. For example, when delivering a presentation at a multilingual conference, providing headsets for simultaneous translation can substantially affect how your message is received and understood.

Tailoring your content to reflect local interests and issues is crucial internationally. This adaptation involves more than translating your speech; it's about recontextualizing your message to align with regional perspectives and concerns. Research local issues, market trends, and cultural stories that can be woven into your presentation to make it more relevant and engaging. For instance, if discussing renewable energy in a region significantly impacted by environmental changes, incorporate local ecological data and reference ongoing local initiatives. This increases the relatability of your content and enhances your credibility as a speaker who is well-informed and considerate of the audience's context.

As discussed in Chapter 4, humor can be a powerful tool in public speaking; however, navigating humor across different cultures can be tricky. What is thought of as humorous in one culture can be offensive or bewildering in another. When integrating humor into your speech, choose universal themes likely to resonate across cultures. Test these elements during the preparation phase with individuals from the target culture to gauge their appropriateness and effectiveness. Similarly, when using examples or anecdotes, ensure they are culturally relatable and do not rely on specific cultural knowledge your international audience might not share.

Incorporating humor and culturally relevant examples lightens the mood, enhances engagement, and bridges cultural gaps, making your presentation a memorable experience that resonates globally. By carefully selecting and tailoring these elements, you ensure that your international presentations are understood, appreciated, and remembered across cultural boundaries.

## 10.2 PUBLIC SPEAKING FOR EDUCATIONAL SETTINGS

Educational settings present a unique challenge and opportunity for public speakers. Here, you are not just a speaker but a facilitator of learning tasked with engaging a potentially diverse group of learners. Addressing how individuals absorb and process information is crucial to connecting with all students effectively. This means crafting presentations that cater to visual, auditory, and kinesthetic learners. Visual learners benefit significantly from using well-designed slides, infographics, and diagrams illustrating key points. For these students, visual aids are not just enhancements; they are essential components that help clarify and retain new information.

On the other hand, auditory learners focus on the spoken words and the nuances of tone and pitch. A well-structured speech with clear enunciation can amplify understanding, perhaps supplemented by audio clips. Lastly, kinesthetic learners thrive on action and interaction. Incorporating activities that allow these students to physically engage with the material—such as building models, performing role-play, or even simple tasks like writing or drawing during the session—can boost their learning efficacy.

Beyond catering to different learning styles, the structure of your presentation in an educational setting can influence the effectiveness of your delivery. It's beneficial to segment your topic into clearly defined chunks, each focused on a single aspect of the subject matter. This approach maintains clarity and focus while aiding learners in mentally processing and structuring information. Regular summarization points are required; they serve as mental 'breathing spaces,' allowing students to integrate what they've learned before moving on to new information.

Including interactive techniques can transform a static lecture into a dynamic learning experience. Techniques such as real-time Q&A sessions encourage active participation and allow speakers to address students' queries as they arise, which can clarify doubts and deepen understanding. Group discussions are another powerful tool; they foster peer learning and increase student communication skills. Moreover, hands-on activities related to the topic can make the learning experience more tangible and memorable. For example, demonstrating physics principles through live experiments can transform abstract concepts into tangible, understandable ideas. These hands-on elements make the learning process more engaging and effective, turning students from passive recipients of information into active participants in their educational journey.

Lastly, evaluating the understanding of your audience is crucial in educational settings. This assessment should be more comprehensive than formal tests or quizzes at the end of your presentation. Enhance engagement by integrating instant feedback tools such as electronic polls or interactive apps, allowing students to provide anonymous input during the session. This helps gauge their grasp of the material in real-time and allows you to adjust your pace and approach if necessary. Informal feedback sessions, where students discuss what they've learned or express areas of confusion, can also provide insights into their understanding and retention. Adjusting your presentation based on this feedback is vital; it demonstrates responsiveness to your audience's needs and the learning experience, ensuring your educational objectives are successfully met.

By integrating these strategies—catering to diverse learning styles, structuring content for educational impact, employing interactive techniques, and evaluating understanding—you ensure that your presentations are informative and transformative educational experiences. These practices foster an environment where learning is engaging and dynamic, encouraging students to explore, question, and understand the world around them more profoundly and meaningfully.


## 10.3 CORPORATE SPEECHES: ENGAGING STAKEHOLDERS

When stepping into the corporate arena to deliver a speech, the stakes are invariably high, and the audience comprises key stakeholders—investors, employees, partners, and possibly the media. Each of these groups comes with distinct expectations and objectives. For instance, investors might focus on the return on their investments, employees on how company strategies affect their job security and work environment, and partners may be interested in long-term business strategies and their alignment with their goals. Understanding these varied perspectives is crucial. Before crafting your speech, invest time in identifying these objectives through discussions, surveys, or feedback from previous interactions. This preparatory step enables you to tailor your message to address specific concerns and interests effectively, ensuring that your speech resonates with each audience segment and meets them at their point of need.

Maintaining a professional tone and demeanor throughout your presentation is essential. The corporate environment demands a formality and sophistication that reflects on you as a speaker and your organization. This professionalism in language and delivery reassures your stakeholders of the seriousness and credibility of the message. Use language that is both respectful and authoritative, steering clear of colloquialisms that might undermine the gravity of your discourse. Your demeanor, too, should exude confidence and composure, qualities that stakeholders respect and expect in leaders. This does not mean your speech should lack warmth or personality—on the contrary, a touch of personal engagement can make your delivery more compelling. However, the overall tone should align with the expectations of a corporate audience, which values clarity, precision, and professionalism.

In the context of corporate speeches, particularly those that deal with financial results, growth strategies, or market analysis, the incorporation of data is invaluable. Charts, graphs, and tables are powerful tools that help clarify your points and provide evidence to support your claims. For example, a well-designed graph can illustrate trends more effectively than verbal descriptions alone when discussing financial results. Similarly, data projections can lend credibility to your proposed initiatives if you outline growth strategies. However, the key is to integrate this data seamlessly into your speech. Each visual element should be directly relevant to the point you are discussing and presented in a way that is easy to understand. Avoid overwhelming your audience with complex data or cluttered visuals. Instead, opt for simplicity and clarity, ensuring each piece of data contributes directly to the narrative of your speech.

Concluding a corporate speech effectively often involves a solid call to action. This presentation element is crucial as it directs your stakeholders toward the desired outcome: rallying support for a new project, encouraging participation in corporate initiatives, or simply reinforcing their engagement with the company.

Your call to action should be clear, compelling, and achievable. For instance, if your goal is to gain buy-in for a new project, your call-to-action might involve inviting stakeholders to a follow-up meeting where they can learn more and express their thoughts. Alternatively, if you seek to boost participation in a corporate initiative, ask stakeholders to sign up or commit to the initiative before leaving the room. Whatever the action you are advocating, ensure it is framed to highlight the benefits to the stakeholders, aligning it with their interests and objectives discussed earlier in your speech. This alignment increases the likelihood of positive responses and reinforces the relevance and urgency of your message.

## 10.4 PUBLIC SPEAKING FOR SOCIAL EVENTS AND CEREMONIES

In the tapestry of public speaking, social events and ceremonies hold a unique place where the spoken word blends with personal touches and shared experiences, all tailored to the specific occasion. Whether it's a joyful wedding toast, a solemn eulogy at a funeral, an enthusiastic announcement at a gala, or a heartfelt speech at a community gathering, the tone and content of your speech can significantly enhance the atmosphere and emotional resonance of the event. Adapting your tone to match the formality or informality of these events is crucial. For a wedding, a light and celebratory tone filled with warmth and humor can uplift the spirit of the occasion. At the same time, a funeral would warrant a more subdued and respectful tone, emphasizing compassion and comfort.

A solution to mastering the tone for different social events is understanding the purpose and the audience's expectations. For instance, a speech at a gala intended to raise funds for a cause could inspire and encourage attendees to open their hearts and wallets. In contrast, a community gathering might benefit from a conversational and inclusive tone, fostering a sense of unity and shared purpose among attendees. To effectively adapt your tone, immerse yourself in the essence of the event beforehand—understand its significance, the audience's emotional state, and the overall atmosphere. This empathy will guide your tone, helping you to strike the right chord with your audience.

Personalizing the content of your speeches for these events is equally important. Incorporating personal stories, anecdotes, or messages that resonate with the specific audience not only personalizes the experience but also deepens the emotional impact of your words. When speaking at a wedding, sharing a memorable story about the couple that highlights their journey or unique qualities can evoke a sense of intimacy and joy. For a funeral, sharing anecdotes that celebrate the life and virtues of the deceased can offer solace and a personal touch that honors their memory. These elements transform your speech from a mere formality into a meaningful contribution to the occasion.

Timing and breathing are critical in social events, where the primary focus is on the celebration or remembrance rather than the speech itself. Keeping your speeches concise and to the point respects the audience's desire to partake in the event. For instance, a wedding toast should be brief enough to maintain the festive mood without overshadowing the other ceremonial elements. Similarly, a speech at a community event should be concise, allowing ample time for interaction and participation from the community members. To master the art of brevity, focus on your main message and eliminate any extraneous content. Practice delivering your speech to ensure it fits within the appropriate time frame, making every word count towards the overarching message of the occasion.

Emotional content requires a delicate balance between expressing genuine emotions and composure to deliver your speech effectively. This is particularly pertinent in ceremonies like funerals or heartfelt tributes, where emotions run high. To manage this, prepare thoroughly by reflecting on what you want to convey and practicing your speech to foster emotional stability. Allow yourself to experience and process these emotions during preparation to share them with poise during the event. Techniques such as pausing after a particularly emotional point can give both you and your audience a moment to absorb the sentiment, maintaining a connection that supports the event's purpose without being overwhelmed by emotion.

In these social settings, your speech becomes a bridge that connects personal stories and communal experiences, enriching the event with memories and messages that resonate with all present. As you weave these elements together, your speech commemorates the occasion and enhances the collective experience, leaving a lasting impact beyond words.

As we close this chapter on adapting public speaking to various particular contexts and audiences, we see how flexibility, empathy, and a deep understanding of the audience's needs and expectations shape the effectiveness of your communication. Whether addressing an international conference, leading an educational seminar, delivering a corporate presentation, or speaking at a social event, the principles of tailored content, appropriate tone, and audience engagement remain constant. These skills are tools for effective communication and bridges to deeper connections and understanding across diverse contexts.

Looking forward, the next chapter delves into innovative techniques and emerging trends in public speaking to keep you at the forefront of this dynamically evolving field. By embracing these advancements, you continue to refine your skills and adapt to the changing communication landscapes, prepared to meet the future with confidence and eloquence.

# CHAPTER ELEVEN

# INNOVATION AND TRENDS IN PUBLIC SPEAKING

Picture yourself at the confluence of time-honored tradition and cutting-edge technology, where the venerable art of oratory converges with the ever-evolving realm of digital innovation. This juncture isn't merely a point of contact; it's a springboard catapulting public speaking into previously uncharted territories. As we navigate this chapter, we'll explore how the digital age has reshaped the landscape of public speaking, transforming it from its classical roots into a vibrant, interactive multimedia experience.

We'll delve into the revolutionary impact of virtual and augmented reality on presentations, examining how these technologies are creating immersive experiences that transcend physical boundaries. You'll discover how artificial intelligence is revolutionizing public speaking training, offering personalized feedback and enhancing practice sessions in previously impossible ways.

But our journey continues beyond current innovations. We'll gaze forward, contemplating the trends shaping the next generation of public speakers. From holographic presentations to neuro-linguistic programming advancements, we'll explore the cutting edge of communication technology and its potential to redefine how we connect with audiences.

By the end of this chapter, you'll have a comprehensive understanding of the technological landscape shaping modern public speaking. You'll be equipped not just to adapt to these changes but to harness them, positioning yourself at the forefront of innovation in public communication.

Following the main content, you'll find a set of forward-thinking exercises designed to help you engage with these emerging technologies and trends. These activities will challenge you to think creatively about the future of public speaking and how to integrate innovative approaches into your practice.

## 11.1 THE EVOLUTION OF PUBLIC SPEAKING IN THE DIGITAL ERA

The history of public speaking stretches back to ancient times when orators in Athens and Rome swayed the masses and shaped the foundations of democracy with nothing but their words and conviction. Fast-forward to the 20th century, when the advent of radio and television shifted public speaking from the physical podiums to broadcast studios, expanding the audience reach but still limiting interaction. However, the true transformation began with the rise of the internet and digital technology, which have democratized public speaking in unprecedented ways.

Introducing visual aids, from simple slideshows to complex multimedia presentations, marked one of the first milestones in integrating technology into public speaking. This evolution continued with the advent of online platforms where webinars and virtual conferences have become commonplace. Today, social media platforms have taken this further by integrating live streaming, enabling speakers to reach global audiences instantly. Each technological advancement has expanded the reach of public speakers and enhanced how messages are delivered and received.

The impact of digital communication on public speaking is profound. Audiences today expect more than just a monologue; they seek an interactive experience that engages them on multiple levels. Digital tools have risen to this challenge by enabling dynamic interactions through real-time polls, Q&A sessions, and social media integration. This shift has encouraged speakers to transform their presentations into two-way conversations with their audience, making each session more engaging and personalized. For instance, integrating Twitter feeds into presentations allows speakers to receive and respond to audience feedback live, creating a more engaging and responsive speaking experience.

However, this transformation has its challenges. The digital era is also distraction-rich, where speakers must compete with the constant buzz of smartphones, social media notifications, and their audiences' ever-shortening attention spans. Yet, these challenges also present unique opportunities. Incorporate interactive infographics that audiences can explore through their devices, enhancing engagement and data comprehension. Speakers can turn potential distractions into engagement tools. These digital innovations keep the audience engaged and enhance the retention of information by involving them actively in the learning process.

As we continue to delve into the digital transformation of public speaking, it's clear that the journey is as dynamic as the technology driving it. By embracing these innovations, speakers can create more impactful, engaging, and memorable presentations that reach the globe and resonate deeply with every individual in the audience. As you incorporate digital tools into your presentations, focus on how they can elevate your message and transform audience interaction.

## 11.2 VIRTUAL REALITY AND AUGMENTED REALITY IN PRESENTATIONS

As we proceed into digital innovation, two technologies stand out for their profound impact on public speaking and presentations: Virtual Reality (VR) and Augmented Reality (AR). VR immerses users in a completely virtual environment, a simulated world ranging from realistic to fantastical. AR, conversely, layers computer-generated enhancements atop an existing reality, enriching the user's perception of the real world without replacing it. Both technologies offer unique opportunities to transform public speaking from a passive experience into an interactive and immersive journey.

The potential of VR and AR to create captivating presentation experiences is vast. Imagine delivering a lecture on ancient Roman history where, instead of static images, you use VR to transport your audience right into the heart of Rome, strolling through the Forum or the Colosseum as it stood centuries ago. Or consider an AR presentation for a new architectural design, where clients can see and interact with a 3D model of a building superimposed over a real-world plot. These technologies make presentations more engaging and enhance understanding and retention by allowing audiences to experience content in dynamic and interactive ways. Successful implementations of VR and AR in presentations across various sectors—from education and training to marketing and design—demonstrate their effectiveness in engaging audiences profoundly and memorably.

Various tools and platforms are available for public speakers and presenters eager to incorporate virtual reality (VR) and augmented reality (AR) into public speaking and presentations:

1. **Virtual Orator:** This VR simulator allows users to practice public speaking in realistic virtual environments. It offers customizable settings for venue, audience size, and behavior, helping speakers overcome anxiety and refine their skills.

2. **Meta Quest VR headsets:** These devices can create immersive presentation environments or practice speaking in virtual settings.

3. **RayBan Meta Smart Glasses:** These AR glasses can potentially display information or visual aids during speeches.

4. **JigSpace:** This platform enables detailed augmented reality presentations, including product descriptions. It could help create engaging visual content to accompany speeches.

5. **Xreal AR glasses:** These sleek augmented reality glasses are compatible with various devices and can

display information or visual aids during presentations.

6. **ENGAGE:** This platform runs on various spatial computing devices, including VR, AR, XR, PCs, Mac, iOS, and Android. It offers tools for collaboration, such as immersive whiteboards, screen streaming, 3D virtual pens, and spatial VoIP communications, which could be utilized for interactive presentations or speeches.

When integrating VR and AR into presentations, it's essential to adhere to best practices to ensure that these technologies enhance rather than distract from the message. Start by clearly defining the purpose of using VR or AR. Is it to illustrate a point that would be difficult to convey with traditional slides? Or to provide a hands-on experience that deepens understanding? Once the purpose is clear, design your VR or AR elements as intuitive and user-friendly as possible. Avoid overloading your presentation with unnecessary technological flairs; use VR and AR to complement your narrative, not to overshadow it. Additionally, it's wise to prepare for potential technical glitches by having backup plans such as simplified versions of your VR or AR experiences or traditional slides that can convey your message effectively. This preparation ensures that your presentation can proceed smoothly, regardless of technical challenges.

## 11.3 THE ROLE OF ARTIFICIAL INTELLIGENCE IN PUBLIC SPEAKING TRAINING

As we continue to navigate the evolving landscape of public speaking, artificial intelligence (AI) emerges as a transformative force, reshaping how we deliver speeches and prepare for them. AI-driven training tools are revolutionizing the traditional methodologies of public speaking training, offering a more personalized and efficient approach to skill enhancement. Among the myriad of tools available, speech analysis software stands out. This technology evaluates your speaking performance by providing detailed feedback on pacing, tone, and clarity. Imagine a tool that listens to your rehearsal presentations and then offers tailored advice on modulating your voice for better engagement or adjusting your pacing to enhance clarity. Such feedback is invaluable as it allows for real-time improvements, ensuring delivery is compelling and resonant with your audience.

Personalizing learning experiences through AI is one of the most significant advancements in public speaking training. By analyzing patterns in your speech delivery, AI can identify specific areas that need improvement and suggest customized exercises to address these. For instance, if you tend to speak too quickly, AI can recommend exercises designed to enhance your pacing. Or, if your speeches lack variation in tone, it might suggest techniques to inject more dynamism into your delivery. This personalized coaching is akin to having a personal trainer for public speaking, but one that is deeply attuned to the nuances of your performance. This method makes learning more effective and ensures that the training is aligned with your individual needs, helping you develop a more authentic and impactful speaking style.

Another groundbreaking application of AI in public speaking is real-time language translation. This feature expands the reach of public speakers by allowing them to communicate seamlessly with audiences regardless of language barriers. Imagine delivering a speech in English while AI technology simultaneously translates your words into multiple languages, displaying real-time subtitles or providing translated audio feeds to a global audience. This technology makes public speaking more inclusive and more engaging for international audiences. It democratizes information, ensuring that your message has the most comprehensive possible impact, and allows for a broader exchange of ideas across different cultures and languages.

Integrating AI into public speaking introduces ethical issues that require thorough examination and thoughtful resolution. One of the primary concerns is privacy. AI tools analyze your speech and performance and collect large amounts of data about your speaking style and preferences. Ensuring this data is handled with the utmost respect for privacy and confidentiality is crucial. Moreover, maintaining a genuine human connection in presentations is challenging. While AI can enhance the delivery and reach of your speeches, it is vital to preserve the personal touch that makes public speaking resonate on an emotional level. Balancing the use of AI tools with the need to maintain authenticity in your presentations is vital to ensuring that technology enhances rather than detracts from your message.

As we embrace AI's potential to transform public speaking training, it is essential to navigate these advancements thoughtfully. You can enhance your skills and extend your reach by leveraging AI-driven tools for personalized training and real-time translation. Simultaneously, by being mindful of ethical concerns and striving to keep your presentations genuinely engaging, you ensure that using AI enriches your public speaking endeavors, allowing you to connect with and captivate your audience more effectively than ever before.

## 11.4 FUTURE TRENDS: WHAT'S NEXT FOR PUBLIC SPEAKERS?

As we peer into the horizon of public speaking, a fascinating evolution is underway, shaped by technology and shifting societal norms. One of the most intriguing advancements is the integration of predictive analytics into public speaking. Imagine stepping onto a stage, equipped not just with your speech but also with data-driven insights predicting how your audience might react to each segment of your presentation. Based on past audience reactions, real-time engagement metrics, and social media sentiment analysis, predictive analytics allows speakers to customize their presentations dynamically, ensuring maximum impact. This technology doesn't just anticipate reactions; it provides a roadmap for speakers to adjust their pacing, tone, and content in real-time, transforming a static presentation into an adaptive conversation that resonates deeply with the audience.

The future also heralds an era of increased interactivity in public speaking. The days of passive audiences quietly absorbing hour-long monologues are fading, giving way to a more dynamic interaction where the audience plays an active role in shaping the content. Through technologies like live polling or real-time content customization, speakers can pivot their presentations based on immediate feedback from the audience. This shift makes presentations more engaging and ensures that the content delivered is what the audience finds most valuable and relevant. Imagine a scenario where audience feedback during a presentation leads to a deeper dive into a particularly intriguing topic or prompts a shift to a more fundamental explanation if they're not following—this level of adaptability could redefine the boundaries of effective communication.

Sustainability is becoming increasingly crucial in all sectors, and public speaking is no exception. The environmental cost of hosting large events, including travel and material use, is prompting a shift towards more sustainable practices. Virtual presentations and webinars are becoming the norm, significantly reducing the carbon footprint associated with travel. Moreover, digital handouts and VR environments for virtual attendance continue to decrease reliance on physical materials, making public speaking more eco-friendly. The sustainability trend is not just about reducing impact; it's also about broadening accessibility and allowing global audiences to participate in events from which they might otherwise be excluded due to geographic and economic barriers.

Finally, the evolution of speaker-audience dynamics is reshaping the landscape of public speaking. The traditional model of a speaker as the sole disseminator of information is transforming, with audiences now seeking a more participatory role. This shift is evident in the move towards formats that foster dialogue and discussion, allowing for a two-way exchange of ideas. Speakers are increasingly seen as facilitators of discussion rather than mere providers of information, a trend that encourages deeper engagement and makes the act of public speaking more collaborative and inclusive.

As we look to the future, these trends suggest a vibrant trajectory for public speaking, marked by greater personalization, interactivity, sustainability, and collaboration. These developments promise to enhance public speaking's effectiveness and enrich its role as a tool for education, engagement, and change.

Whether you are a seasoned speaker looking to innovate or a newcomer eager to make your mark, the upcoming insights will provide you with the tools to thrive in the evolving world of public speaking. By staying ahead of these trends, you can ensure that your public speaking keeps pace with the times and sets new standards for effectiveness and impact.

Here are practical exercises for innovating your public speaking journey.

### 1. AR Presentation Enhancement

- Choose a topic you know and create an introductory 5-slide presentation.
- Research AR presentation tools (e.g., Prezi, ARize, Adobe Aero).
- Use one of these tools to add AR elements to your presentation. This could include 3D models, interactive graphs, or virtual environments.
- Present to a small group (in person or virtually), incorporating these AR elements.

- Gather feedback on how the AR elements impacted the audience's understanding and engagement.

## 2. AI-Assisted Speech Analysis

- Record yourself giving a 3-minute speech on any topic.
- Use an AI-powered speech analysis tool (e.g., Yoodli, Orai, or Google's Speech-to-Text API) to analyze your speech.
- Review the AI's pacing, filler words, tone, and clarity feedback.
- Based on this feedback, re-record your speech, consciously working on the areas highlighted by the AI.
- Compare the two versions and reflect on the usefulness of AI feedback in improving your speaking skills.

## 3. Future-Focused Speaking Scenario

- Imagine you're speaking at a conference in 2040. Technology has advanced significantly.
- Write a 1-page description of how you envision delivering a speech in this future scenario. Consider:

  - The venue (physical, virtual, or hybrid?)
  - Audience interaction methods
  - Visual aids and presentation tools
  - Real-time translation capabilities
  - Any other innovative features you can imagine

- ○ Share your vision with a peer and discuss the potential impacts of these innovations on public speaking.

### 4. Tech-Enhanced Mini-Talk

- Choose a topic related to your field of expertise.
- Prepare a 5-minute talk incorporating at least three innovative techniques or technologies discussed in this chapter. This could include:

  - ○ Using VR to create an immersive environment
  - ○ Incorporating AI-generated real-time audience feedback
  - ○ Using holographic visuals
  - ○ Implementing real-time language translation

- Deliver this talk to a small group (in person or virtually).
- After the talk, lead a discussion about the effectiveness of these innovations and how they might shape the future of public speaking.

# KEEPING THE CONVERSATION GOING

Now that you have everything you need to become a confident and effective public speaker, it's time to pass on your newfound knowledge and show other readers where they can find the same help.

Simply by leaving your honest opinion of this book on Amazon, you'll show other aspiring speakers where they can find the information they're looking for, and pass their passion for powerful communication forward.

Thank you for your help. The art of public speaking is kept alive when we share our knowledge – and you're helping me to do just that.

Your review could be the catalyst that helps someone:

- Overcome their fear of public speaking
- Develop a unique and authentic speaking style
- Master the art of engaging any audience
- Adapt to new technologies in presentations
- Advance their career through effective communication

Scan the QR code to leave a review:

Your words could be the encourage-
ment someone needs to take that first
step towards becoming a confident
speaker. By sharing your experience,
you're not just leaving a review; you're
extending a hand to those who are where you once were.

Remember, every great speaker started as a novice. Your
review could be the beginning of someone else's journey to
becoming an inspiring communicator.

Thank you for being part of this community of passionate
communicators. Together, we're amplifying voices and
empowering ideas.

- With gratitude, Grace Lancaster

PS - If this book has made a difference in your public
speaking journey, consider sharing it with a friend or
colleague. Let's keep spreading the power of confident
communication!

* * *

# CONCLUSION

As we draw the curtains on this journey through the intricate and exhilarating world of public speaking, we must reflect on our path together. From understanding the roots of public speaking anxiety to mastering the art of engaging diverse audiences and embracing cutting-edge technologies, your progress has been nothing short of transformative. You've learned the fundamentals of effective communication and how to adapt these skills to the ever-evolving platforms and audiences that define our modern world.

Authenticity and continuous learning stand as pillars in the art of public speaking. Developing a personal style that resonates with truth and engaging in lifelong learning are not merely strategies for success; they are commitments to personal fulfillment and professional excellence. Each speech, each presentation, and each story told is an opportunity to express a unique perspective and connect with others in meaningful ways.

We've revisited key strategies for captivating various audiences, emphasizing the importance of tailoring your messages for different contexts—from corporate boardrooms to social gatherings and international stages. Whether through social media platforms or advanced tools like virtual reality and artificial intelligence, technology has opened new horizons for public speakers to explore and conquer.

The significance of practice cannot be overstated. Each presentation you give is a step forward in your journey, with feedback serving as your compass. The practice, reception, and refinement cycle is essential for growth and mastery in public speaking. Embrace this cycle with enthusiasm and openness, knowing each iteration enhances your skills and sharpens your delivery.

Emerging technologies like virtual reality, augmented reality, and artificial intelligence are not just trends; they are the future landscapes of public speaking. These tools offer unprecedented ways to engage and inspire audiences, making public speaking more dynamic and impactful. I encourage you to explore these avenues and experiment with how these technologies can enhance your presentations and bring your messages to life in ways previously unimaginable.

Please confidently step forward in your public speaking engagements. See each opportunity to speak as a canvas on which to paint your words, a chance to leave an indelible mark on your listeners. Whether it's a small team meeting or a large conference, remember that your journey to excellence in public speaking begins with a single step. Start speaking now, apply your learned techniques, and continue to evolve and adapt.

I invite you to share your successes and challenges with me and others on this same path. By sharing our stories and experiences, we build a community of support and inspiration, encouraging one another as we grow and succeed in public speaking.

Remember that public speaking is a path of endless learning and discovery. Each voice can inspire change, move hearts, and open minds. Embrace this power, and let your voice be heard. Thank you for allowing me to be a part of your journey. Let's continue to speak, share, and inspire together.

# REFERENCES


*Tips & Guides - Dealing with Speech Anxiety - Hamilton College* https://www.hamilton.edu/academics/centers/oralcommunication/guides/dealing-with-speech-anxiety

*Powerful Storytelling for Public Speakers* https://projectcharisma.com/storytelling-for-public-speakers-guide/

*Gestures and Body Language - Toastmasters International* https://www.toastmasters.org/resources/public-speaking-tips/gestures-and-body-language

*10 Proven Virtual Event Speaker Engagement Strategies To Captivate Your Audience* https://www.beaconlive.com/blog/10-proven-virtual-event-speaker-engagement-strategies-to-captivate-your-audience-beaconlive

*Tips & Guides - Dealing with Speech Anxiety - Hamilton College* https://www.hamilton.edu/academics/centers/oralcommunication/guides/dealing-with-speech-anxiety

*Cognitive behavioral therapy for public-speaking anxiety ...* https://pubmed.ncbi.nlm.nih.gov/16231290/

*The Power of Mindfulness - How It Can Improve Your Public Speaking* https://www.speaking.coach/the-power-of-mindfulness-how-it-can-improve-your-public-speaking/

*Role-Playing - Preparing for Difficult Conversations and ...* https://www.mindtools.com/acjtx9g/role-playing

*The six rules of impactful PowerPoint design.* https://buffalo7.co.uk/blog/powerpoint-design-rules/

*The PREP Framework : An Easy Way to Give Excellent Impromptu Speeches* https://kennethmd.com/the-prep-framework-an-easy-way-to-give-excellent-impromptu-speeches/

*Audience Analysis | Department of Communication* https://www.comm.pitt.edu/oral-comm-lab/audience-analysis

*Help! How Can I Memorize My Speeches? - ModernBrain* https://www.modernbrain.com/blog/how-to-memorize-my-speech

*Handling the Q&A Session With Confidence* https://www.toastmasters.org/magazine/magazine-issues/2021/mar/handling-the-qanda-session-with-confidence

*17 Impactful Persuasive Techniques to Become a Master ...* https://www.even tible.com/learning/persuasive-techniques/

*THE ETHICAL OBLIGATIONS OF A PUBLIC SPEAKER* https://communica tion.ecu.edu/cce/2022/08/30/ethical-obligations/

*How VR can Improve your Public Speaking Skills* https://virtualspeech.com/ blog/using-vr-to-improve-public-speaking-skills

*13 Webinar Engagement Strategies to Keep Your ...* https://www.vfairs.com/ blog/webinar-engagement-strategies/

*How to plan a successful social media content strategy for ...* https://pibworthps. com/social-media-content-strategy-for-speakers/

*Presentation tips for handling technical difficulties - Microsoft* https://www. microsoft.com/en-us/microsoft-365-life-hacks/presentations/how-to-handle-presentation-interruptions-or-technical-difficulties

*15 Tips for Effective Communication in Leadership | CCL* https://www.ccl.org/ articles/leading-effectively-articles/communication-1-idea-3-facts-5-tips/

*Let's Talk: Crafting an effective elevator pitch* https://dynamicbusiness.com/ leadership-2/lets-talk-business/lets-talk-crafting-an-effective-elevator-pitch.html#:

*10 Tips to Handle Difficult Questions During Your Presentation* https://www. johnmillen.com/blog/10-tips-to-handle-difficult-questions-during-a-presentation

*5 Key Strategies for Effective Cross-Cultural Communication* https://msquareme dia.com/5-key-strategies-for-effective-cross-cultural-communication/

*7 Proven Storytelling Techniques to Captivate Your Audience in Public Speaking* https://blog.daisie.com/7-proven-storytelling-techniques-to-captivate-your-audience-in-public-speaking/

*7 Top Tips To Master Virtual Audience Engagement And Keep Them Hooked* https://www.moxieinstitute.com/7-top-tips-to-master-virtual-audi ence-engagement-and-keep-them-hooked/

*Embodied strategies for public speaking anxiety* https://www.ncbi.nlm.nih.gov/ pmc/articles/PMC10711069/

*Rhetorical Analysis of Martin Luther King Jr's 'I have a ...* https://us.ukessays. com/essays/english-language/rhetorical-analysis-of-martin-luther-king-jrs-i-have-a-dream-speech-2237.php

*How to Become an Authentic Speaker* https://hbr.org/2008/11/how-to-become-an-authentic-speaker

*12 Easy 5-Minute Vocal Exercises to Improve Your Speech* https://yoodli.ai/blog/ 5-minute-voice-exercises-for-speaking

*Social Psychological Face Perception: Why Appearance ...* https://www.ncbi.nlm.nih.gov/pmc/articles/PMC2811283/

*How To Master Audience Engagement When You Present* https://www.duarte.com/audience-engagement-strategies-presentations/

*Structure Your Presentation Like a Story* https://hbr.org/2012/10/structure-your-presentation-li

*10 Cutting-Edge Technologies to Enhance Audience Engagement at Live Events* https://createengage.com.au/10-cutting-edge-technologies-to-enhance-audience-engagement-at-live-events/#:

*Ten Simple Rules for Running Interactive Workshops - PMC* https://www.ncbi.nlm.nih.gov/pmc/articles/PMC3937100/

*Augmented Reality in Education & Training: Use Cases and ...* https://www.fingent.com/blog/augmented-reality-in-education-training-use-cases-and-business-benefits/

*Impact of AI in Public Speaking with Generative AI - LinkedIn* https://www.linkedin.com/pulse/impact-ai-public-speaking-generative-dr-hemachandran-k-i88yc

*10 Proven Virtual Event Speaker Engagement Strategies ...* https://www.beaconlive.com/blog/10-proven-virtual-event-speaker-engagement-strategies-to-captivate-your-audience-beaconlive

*How to Use Social Media as a Thought Leader* https://www.linkedin.com/advice/0/how-can-thought-leaders-use-social-media-increase-mdgmf

*How to write a great speech for your CEO in 2024. https://prnomics.com/how-to-write-a-great-speech-for-your-ceo-in-2024/*

*Resumes/CVs, LinkedIn Profiles & More: Your Complete Guide. https://www.bluesteps.com/guide-resumescvs-linkedin-profiles-more-your-complete-guide*

*Nelson Mandela Research Paper Topics - iResearchNet.*

*Dervin, D. (2014). The Family Romance of the Group's Political Delegate. The Journal of Psychohistory, 42(2), 147-160.*

*Elevate Your Delivery – Unleash the Power of Teleprompter Services – Green Synthesis.* https://www.crossfitgenesis.com/elevate-your-delivery-unleash-the-power-of-teleprompter-services.htm

*Unleashing the Power of Storytelling: The Secret to Captivating MSP/BSP Marketing Success - Evolved Office.* https://evolvedoffice.com/blog/unleashing-the-power-of-storytelling-the-secret-to-captivating-msp-bsp-marketing-success/

*Rule of Three | Oinam Notes.* https://notes.oinam.com/writing/rule-of-three/

*Syntactical devices, John Renzullo - Coggle Diagram.* https://coggle.it/diagram/Yd8oPPKhpzyjI8qH/t/syntactical-devices

*A Simple Hack to Help You Communicate More Effectively | AAPL Publication.* https://www.physicianleaders.org/articles/a-simple-hack-to-help-you-communicate-more-effectively

*Improving Public Speaking & Presenting Skills 17th MAR 2024 – Business Consultancy and Coaching.* https://vybewoman.com/product/improving-public-speaking-presenting-skills/

*How to Master the Art of Public Speaking: Tips for Overcoming Stage Fright – Totally Questions.* https://totallyquestions.com/how-to-master-the-art-of-public-speaking-tips-for-overcoming-stage-fright/

*How to write a great speech for your CEO in 2024.* https://prnomics.com/how-to-write-a-great-speech-for-your-ceo-in-2024/

*Construction - Communication Skills.* https://www.communicationskills.info/construction/

*Speakers Edge | Life is a Speech.* https://www.lifeisaspeech.com/communicationcoach/services/speakersedge

*8 Science-Backed Ways To Lower Your Stress Right Now - Living Safer Magazine.* https://www.livingsafer.com/8-science-backed-ways-to-lower-your-stress-right-now/

*Adding Comments to JSX | DeveloperMemos.* https://developermemos.com/posts/adding-comments-to-jsx/

*MVP Prototype | Luth Design Studio.* https://www.luth.studio/services/mvp-prototype